BEHIND THE WIRE
Life as a Prisoner of War during WWII

Albert Winter

This book is published by Propagator Press, an imprint of:

AMS Educational
Woodside Trading Estate
Low Lane
Horsforth
Leeds LS18 5NY

© Albert Winter 2005

The rights of Albert Winter. to be identified as the author of this work have been asserted by him in accordance with the Copyright, Designs and Patents Act 1988.

All rights reserved. No part of this publication may be reproduced, stored in a retrieval system, or transmitted in any form or by any means, electronic, mechanical, photocopying, recording or otherwise without the prior written permission of the publishers.

ISBN   1 86029 804 4

Designed by Propagator Press
Printed in Great Britain

Contents

Map of World Convoy and Shipping Routes	4
Map of Routes Travelled 1942-45	5
Preface	6
Introduction	8
Early Days	11
B.E.F. and Dunkirk	13
Back in the UK – The Blitz	25
Liverpool to Egypt (The Long Way Round)	29
To Palestine	32
And So To The Western Desert	35
Forward to Tobruk	41
'In The Bag'	56
Early Days As A PoW	58
Italy	67
Daily Life in Italy	75
Final Days in Italy	91
In German Hands – Moving to Austria	100
In Austria	105
Escapes and Working Camp	121
The Beginning of the End	142
"I'm Free"	150
It All Draws to an End	151
The Last Lap	158
Lingua Franca	161

World Convoy and Shipping Routes

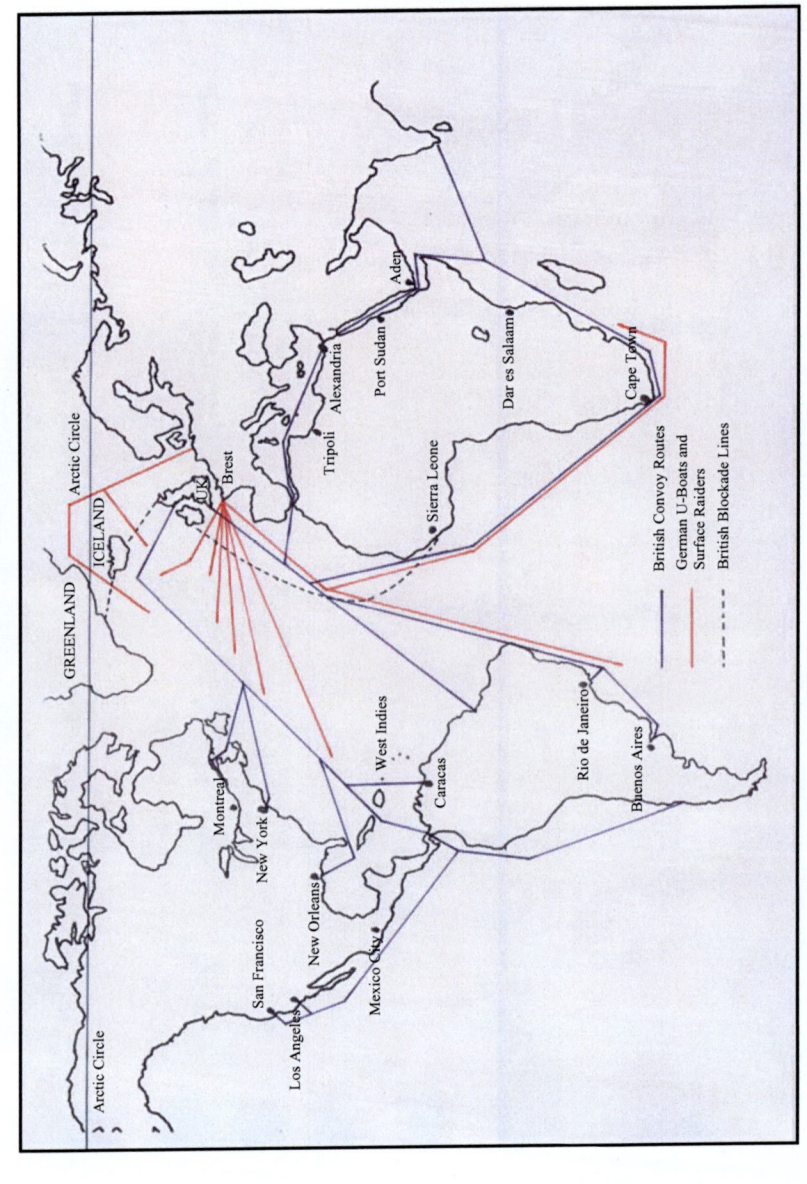

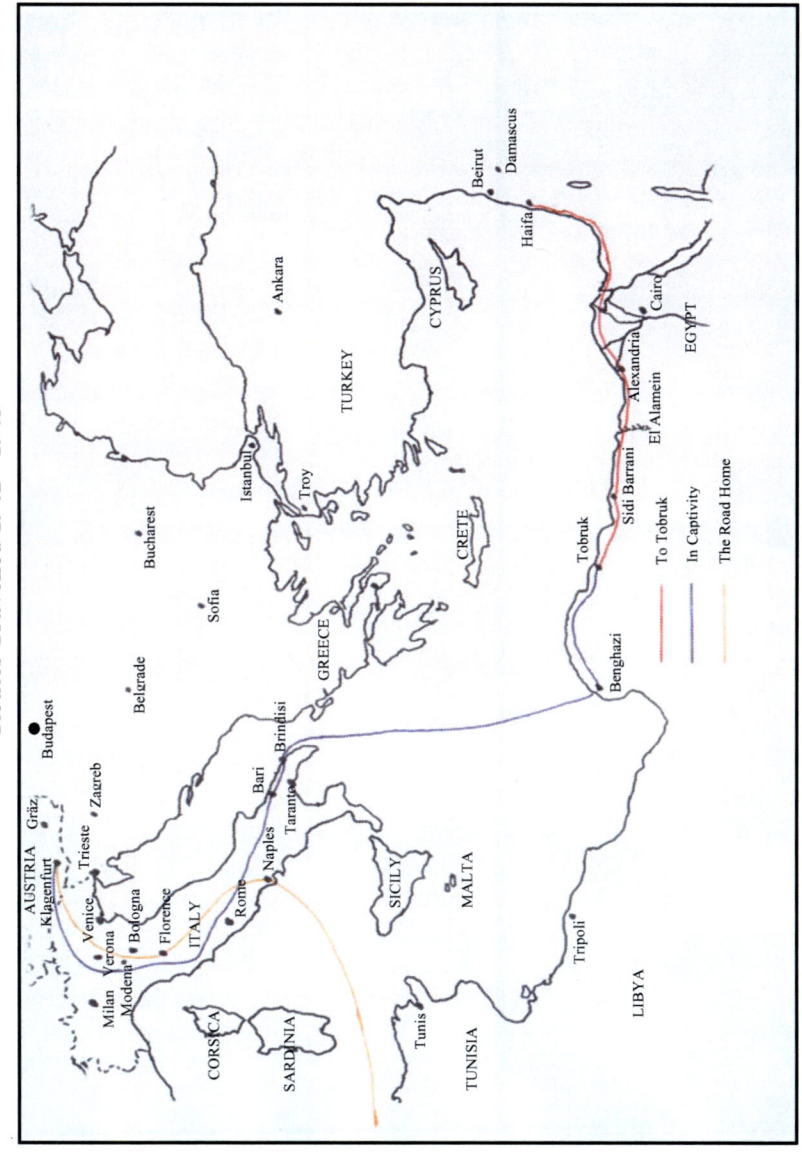

Preface

A few days before the date chosen to celebrate the 60th anniversary of the Second World War on 10th July 2005, my wife and I attended a party proudly wearing our Royal British Legion *V for Victory* badges. We were introduced to a man half my age who, after enquiring where we had obtained the badges, asked me how we could inform those who had been born after 1945 of life during the war years. My simple answer was to tell them to read about it. Days later, Albert asked me to write this preface.

Most war books write about battles or the views of the senior officers who conducted the campaigns. This book is different. You will find no details of the whys and wherefores of the battles in which Albert took part. What you will find is details of the life of a soldier who volunteered to serve King and Country, and the trials and tribulations that came his way. These have moulded the many years with which he has been blessed since the opening of the prisoner of war camp gates in 1945.

Most obituaries to those decorated for their brave actions in war concentrate on the heroic action, with only brief references to the rest of their service. But were they heroes just because of that action? Were they not heroes because of what they went through in the dark days of war – the highs and the lows? When you have read this book, you will know that, for better or for worse, they were heroes just for being there.

Any officer worth his salt knows that when he is first commissioned he has to rely greatly on his sergeant. Some sergeants think they run the army – some do! Albert went to war as a sergeant and, because being taken prisoner ended his career, he finished the war as a sergeant (albeit a senior one!). All the abilities that enable a sergeant to 'run the army' are to be found in these pages. He learnt when to command, when to persuade, when to provide a shoulder to cry on and, above all, to set a good-humoured example. Not easy when you are also feeling fear, anger, hunger and despair – but the sign of a true hero. You will find this for yourself here.

What you do not find, is what Albert did with the rest of his life, when he could choose what he wanted to do; not what he was ordered, bullied or even terrorised into doing. Suffice to say that the experience he gained in war enabled him to face the future with confidence, and to be an example to others from all walks of life. He was rewarded for his selfless work, providing an opportunity for the young to achieve in life as he had done, by his appointment as a Member of the British Empire. But maybe that will be Book Two!

Colonel I. Geoffrey Norton TD JP DL
The York and Lancaster Regiment

Introduction

As Chairman of the Sheffield Dunkirk Veterans' Association, I was invited by Jack Shaw to be interviewed on B.B.C. Radio Sheffield to talk to its listeners of my experiences during World War II.

Appropriately, the interview took place on the morning of Remembrance Sunday 2000. At the end of the interview, Jack stressed to me: "You should write down your wartime experiences for posterity."

On my return to 'Civvy Street' in 1946, I had made notes, but knowing there were like myself, innumerable ex-servicemen who, while serving in many parts of the world had had many interesting experiences but were reluctant to recall them in print, I took the view that people would say, to use a good old service phrase, "He's shooting a line." So the notes were placed in a drawer, to be forgotten.

Now, after Jack Shaw's urging, together with similar requests from friends, I have decided to write my story. I have brought those faded notes out of the drawer where they have been tucked away for almost 60 years. I now have to delve into my memory. A memory that with the passing years is beginning to fray a little at the edges.

Every story has to have a title. During my wartime service I spent three years as a Prisoner of War in Italy and Germany where we were most definitely, 'behind the wire'. The wire was always there, it was never out of sight, whichever way we turned, night and day. It was an eternal reminder that our fate lay in the hands of others, and we were bereft of any decision-making for ourselves. Therefore the title "TALES FROM BEHIND THE WIRE" was not a difficult one to conjure up.

To keep our spirits up during captivity, we spent many hours swapping stories of the various campaigns in which we had fought. Whatever situation we were in, and however disagreeable the conditions we were enduring, one thing which came shining through the gloom was the indomitable British sense of humour. There would always be some 'wit', with a few well-chosen and perfectly timed words, who would change our moments of despair to overwhelming humour. I always tried to have that type of character around me.

The development of real humour came during the early days of our prisoner of war life in southern Italy. We would often get together to deliberate on the ways and means of how to attain and maintain our moral ascendancy over our Italian captors.

Many years have passed since I spent those three vital years of my life as a prisoner of war. With the benefit of hindsight I now realise that those three years were to be invaluable in shaping my character and in giving me a unique insight into human nature. I watched as a constant kaleidoscope of events moved before my eyes and listened, sometimes participating in events myself, but always feeling that I was present as exciting pages of history were being turned. Nowadays while reading history, a subject that has always fascinated me, I can immerse myself once more in that kaleidoscope, and it therefore becomes more real.

In those hectic days of 1940 to 1945, events often merged into one another in such a confused tangle, that some have doubtless drifted out of my memory forever, whilst others are as crystal clear as if they had occurred only yesterday. As I write these words, I feel I have experienced it all before, even though the recollection is getting dimmer and dimmer, so now is the time to write it all down before it is lost forever.

I believe that having experienced a full measure of life's ups and downs, I am certainly a better man for the experiences I have lived through. The thread that is constant throughout the whole gamut is man's inhumanity to man. Sadly, this will never change, especially during the futility of war. Cynical as this may appear, this attitude is forged not by reading books by a cosy fireside, but by personal experience.

Fig: 1 March 1941. The author. Aged 21.

Fig: 2 The author. 2004

Early Days

So to the beginning.

In the pre-war days of the 30s I was always interested in international affairs, and in conversations with my father, who was an avid historian, we became convinced that as a result of what was happening with the re-arming of Hitler's Germany, war was inevitable. Consequently, as it was obvious I would finish up in uniform, I decided to join a T.A. unit to serve among friends.

In December 1938, as a young man of 20, I joined the 9th Army Field Workshop. At that time I was fitter than most of my friends who had enlisted with me, as I had been a keen walker, striding over the Derbyshire moors as often as possible. I was also an avid map-reader, which I believed would be to my advantage when in uniform.

At Whitsuntide in 1939, the T.A. Camp was held at Totley Rifle Range near Sheffield. Having always wanted to fire a .303 rifle, I hoped I would now get the opportunity, but I seemed to spend most of the time rolling and unfurling my 'puttees' (a relic from the first World War, these were wrapped around the ankles, covering the gap between trouser bottoms and boot tops), and having to correctly (in accordance with Army Regulations), lay out my blankets in the bell tents we occupied.

Intent on keeping fit I had rarely drunk beer before joining the TA. At the camp, I was astonished to discover almost everyone drinking what appeared to me enormous quantities of the stuff, and in trying to emulate these apparently hardened drinkers my stomach took a severe beating in those early days.

A few months after the camp at Totley we had been drafted to France and I was promoted to Sergeant in the 51st Highland Division. There I was further encouraged to drink even larger quantities of beer, until I finished up slumped under the table. In the expectations of those days, I had been duly initiated in becoming a soldier.

Back to the T.A., I lined up on the firing range, waiting my turn to fire five rounds of ammunition from a .303 rifle. The Sergeant who was reading out the nominal roll had reached the 'W's for Winter when the Quartermaster came to me saying, "Sorry Winter we have run out of ammunition." "When do we get fresh ammo?" I said. "God only knows" came the gloomy reply. I felt cheated. Like many others, when I eventually first fired 'one up the spout', the Germans were almost on the top of us. So much for a highly trained army!

Even in those early days I wondered what would happen when the chips were really down. I can recollect that when I returned to England still clutching my rifle after the maelstrom of Dunkirk, we were regarded as heroes, and to read the unbelievable accounts in the British press, I felt that I must have taken part in a totally different battle. There were to be many other equally puzzling episodes as the years rolled by.

Still with the T.A., we were billeted at Norbury Hall in Sheffield. As several units were already there we were moved on to Abbeydale Hall in the city suburbs. This was an ideal location surrounded by extensive open spaces. The Orderly Room staff, of which I was a member, were allocated a room on the ground floor of the Hall. This became the Administrative Centre of our unit during the day and served as our sleeping quarters at night. We slept tightly packed together on straw palliasses.

To keep ourselves fit we ran daily around the Hall's grounds. In one of the outbuildings was a room with a large circular stone bath which was used by the players of the local Rugby Club after their matches. Returning from our runs, Sergeant Major Froggatt would stand by the entrance checking that everyone jumped in for a communal bath. This was a shock for many of the young lads who had never exposed themselves before. They would arrive to be greeted by the Sergeant bellowing "Shorts off and get in the water." The timid ones would strip off and hold their hands over their groins, at which the Sergeant Major would roar, "Hands over your heads." This was among the first of many rude shocks they would encounter in the months that lay ahead. No false modesty for the future.

The B.E.F. and Dunkirk

In December 1939, orders finally came through for our unit to move. This was supposed to be a secret, but as we marched down to Dore Railway Station crowds of wives and girlfriends lined our route to bid us all a tearful farewell. Our vehicles, which had gone ahead by road, met us at Aldershot. On arrival we were addressed by a senior Staff Officer who announced that we should be proud that we were joining the famous and battle-hardened 51st Highland Division. Groans went up as someone pointed out that casualties were usually higher in 'famous infantry divisions'.

We travelled by train to Southampton where our troopship was moored alongside a freighter loading military equipment destined for Finland, whose troops were defending their country against a huge Russian invading army. It was a salutary reminder that we were now involved in a global war.

We disembarked at Le Havre. It was a bitter winter in 1939/40 and there was heavy snow all around as we staggered to the railway station, loaded down with our heavy packs, two blankets on top, gas mask, rifle and ammunition, to be pushed into decrepit railway carriages. Sitting in overcoats with our packs on our knees, we glared through the windows at the snow-covered landscape as the train crawled along, falling around as it kept stopping and starting all the way to our destination in the village of St. Pol, not far from Arras. We were billeted in barns and stayed there until the fateful day of 10th May 1940. After what had been a 'phoney war' for several months, this was to be the day when the 'real war' started.

I had been promoted to Sergeant a couple of months previously. One morning at about 5.00 a.m., I was awakened by the roar of aircraft as groups of German bombers flew over us. We were suddenly scrambling to get into our trousers, while trying to keep our heads down at the same time. Utter confusion reigned in the camp for several days. However, we quickly learned that the first lesson in army survival was to get ourselves quickly below ground level for safety when the air raid warning was sounded.

Some days later we were moving north and had crossed the border into Belgium when some 'wag' said "Brussels here we come." We were positioned near the town of Poperinge when the Germans carried out a very heavy air attack on the town, which was an important road junction.

We were hidden in woods but we soon realised we were not safe enough, as we observed a cluster of bombs hurtling down towards us. Fortunately they fell short, the last one landing on a nearby farmhouse. The officer in charge, Colonel Levesley, said to me, "Take a party, Sergeant, and find out if there are any casualties in the farmhouse and see if we can give any medical help."

With the dust still settling, we approached the building where there had been considerable damage to the front. Moving to the front of the farmhouse, I started to push open the shattered door, which was jammed and took some strength to open. As I looked down I saw blood seeping around my boots. Walking into the room I looked down at a dead young Belgian girl, whose body had been ripped apart by the bomb blast. The Medical Orderly following behind me asked, "What's the trouble?" I said, "We can't give any help here." When he saw the body of the girl, he let out a cry and went outside where he was violently sick. I thought to myself, 'He's going to have a hard time as a Medical Orderly.' This was the first dead body I had seen in the war.

Although I was to be constantly shaken by the sight of death in the future, it affected me less and less each time. Eventually one consoles oneself with the thought 'at least I am lucky it is not me.' This bolsters up the courage and dampens down the natural feeling of fear.

I recollected that only a few days previously, as we were ready to move from Armentierres, we had seen no action, only being aware of the rumbling of gunfire in the distance. We were now ready to evacuate some factory buildings fronting on to the main road.

As we stood around, idly watching rows of pathetic civilians moving past with all forms of transport loaded with their household belongings, a group of young girls passed by. One of the lads said, "Look, those girls are from the 'Black Cat' (the local brothel), I think we should give them a hand. When we get back home we can say we have helped a brothel on the move." Suddenly a word of command was shouted out, "HALT." It was Captain Richards who had just arrived. "I don't want to be a spoilsport, but you will only go as far as the next bend in the road. I don't want to have to report that some of you deserted the army by going off with a brothel. Just imagine what that would look like in your army records." This took the heat out of a potentially amusing incident, but at least it relieved the all-pervading misery which surrounded us.

Some time later, we were standing around waiting for orders to move when a motor cycle despatch rider appeared, travelling at high speed and expertly negotiating the debris scattered in the road. He braked to a halt in a cloud of dust and, seeing the Colonel, saluted smartly, handing to him an important looking buff-coloured military envelope. We waited with bated breath to receive its contents from the officer and to find out whether we had been nominated to be the rearguard. There was a short anxious silence as he read the missive, then he crumpled the letter and threw it over his shoulder. Preceded by the usual army expletive he shouted, "Headquarters, 3rd Army Corps says – Don't forget to bring the blackout screens with you."

Finally, we were relieved to receive orders to move away from Poperinge as the town was now the target for very heavy bombing by the German Air Force.

We tried to move as much equipment and as many men as possible at night and finally arrived at Bergues, a walled town on what was to become the perimeter defence of Dunkirk. Here we established ourselves while waiting for further instructions. It was a traumatic time, having to watch our army in retreat. The faces of some of the men passing had a phlegmatic look about them, while others were just terror-stricken. In the distance the faint but ever present sound of gunfire could be heard, accompanied by the recurring sound of bomb explosions.

We were bedded down for the night in a large comfortable hollow around the walls of the town. We later found the hollow to be an old moat surrounding the battlements. Just before dawn we were aroused and ordered to move off quickly and, as we did, water began to lap round our ankles together with an awful stench. We realised that some sewers had been opened to flood the moat. We thought this would be an ingenious way of halting a Panzer Division. That was a perfect example of confused and blockheaded thinking at that panic-stricken time. It was no wonder the Germans were able to advance so swiftly. The whole German military machine had been training for such an attack for years, while we were literally 'babes in arms'.

A few miles from Dunkirk we were ordered to destroy everything except our rifles, and to march in groups towards Dunkirk. Driving our trucks into fields we revved up the engines until they seized, then filled the petrol tanks with sand. Other vehicles we set on fire. It was heartbreaking for the mechanics, who had so lovingly maintained them. At that time, the Territorial Army were only supplied with old regular army vehicles, which required great efforts from the mechanics to keep running efficiently.

All around us similar actions were taking place in other units. What became so confusing was the terrific speed with which all this was happening. We made our way in the dark in the general direction of Dunkirk, which we understood lay about eight miles away. The harbour and all the oil tanks were ablaze, the glow from them lighting up the sky ahead. There was complete silence among us as we trudged along, dispirited, wondering what encounter lay ahead for us.

Fig: 3. The Junkers JU87 'Stuka' dive bomber, used to such devastating effect during the German onslaught on France and over the Dunkirk beaches. Though it was later found to be extremely vulnerable to fighter attack, it was one of the few aircraft to serve throughout WWII.

As dawn broke, we arrived at a point on the coast east of Dunkirk, just beyond the Belgian border outside a town called De Panne, where an increasing number of British troops were assembling, and the English Channel lay before us! To our tired eyes it looked beautiful, but with only a few vessels loading troops, we realised we were going to have to be funnelled through a narrow area which was already subject to heavy attacks by the German Army and Air Force. We realised that it was going to be a long hazardous trip across the Channel before reaching the White Cliffs of Dover, and England.

I was among a group of Sergeants standing about discussing our chances, when we were approached by a Captain who said, "You Sergeants, follow me," which we did and gathered round him in the sand dunes. I soon realised this place to be the Headquarters of the Naval Embarkation Staff. A Naval Officer with a powerful personality and strong voice said to us, "We are going to organise this rabble into orderly queues. I am relying on you men to play your part. There will be four Sergeants to each queue. "Two of you in the water to control the loading of the boats and stop any chance of them being swamped, and two on the foreshore to regulate the lines. I shall visit you every two hours. You will be provided with hot rations this evening." Having had very little to eat over the last two days, this promise was very important to us.

In the first hour or two the organisation appeared to work very well. We congratulated ourselves on being able to bring order out of chaos, as we shepherded the long lines of men into small boats, to be transferred onto larger vessels standing just off shore. All this appeared to be too good to be true. Suddenly there was a concentrated heavy air attack as groups of Messerschmitt fighters swooped low over the dunes, raking the lines of waiting men with machine gun fire.

All hell was suddenly let loose as hundreds of men came splashing back out of the sea vainly trying to dodge the perilous machine gun bullets whistling all around. Today I vividly recall my bursting lungs as I raced across the soft sand for the shelter of the dunes and felt the nearness of the bullets streaking overhead. I flung myself into a hollow as the planes now came down from the opposite direction. Once more the air was full of the sound of the screaming aero engines and the rat-a-tat of machine guns. In a few minutes it was all over and an eerie silence descended.

Fig: 4. Burned out lorry on the beach at Dunkirk. Great efforts were made by the British Army to destroy, or to damage beyond repair, vehicles and weapons which were abandoned on the beaches or the approaches to Dunkirk.

Fig: 5. Troops on the open beach firing back at attacking aircraft.

Then heads began to be raised from the dunes to survey the terrifying scene that met them. Bodies were lying all over the beach, some in lines where machine gun fire had cut like a scythe through the crowds of men. Some of the wounded were dragging themselves towards the dunes, fearful of yet another attack, while moans and groans from others who could not move were mingled with the shouts of, "Stretcher Bearer." A few had made their way to the water's edge, gradually being followed by others. Within ten minutes the scenes of carnage had been almost forgotten as the pushing and jostling to board boats began again.

For the next half-hour we managed, with difficulty, to keep control. A further air attack took place and the dash for the dunes was repeated. New problems now arose when the line reformed, as the pushing and jostling was getting more and more out of control. We four Sergeants were finding it almost impossible to establish discipline. Many of the troops, never having seen enemy action before, had completely lost their nerves. The situation sorted itself out when a further air attack – they were now becoming relentless – took place, followed by a frenzied surge for the boats as soon as the planes had departed. To add to the confusion, the German Stukas had bombed a naval destroyer, which was loading men. Clouds of water and spray had enveloped the destroyer, which was retaliating with its pom-pom guns. When the air cleared we saw the destroyer battered but still afloat. The small boats close by and full to the gunwales with troops, were now just scattered pieces of wreckage. Only a few men could possibly have survived.

The queues to get on boats began to form again. It now became a situation of raw survival and every man for himself. Even before the

Stukas had disappeared, men were dashing to get to the head of the queue before the next attack. Having seen another destroyer closing in, men were fighting to get aboard a boat to take them out to her. Seamen were attempting to push some men off the side of the boat to which they were clinging. It was all in vain and soon the boat capsized, flinging everyone into the water. I was on duty at the water's edge and a witness to the turmoil going on. I and other members of my party rushed forward to give assistance but we were fighting a losing battle.

On reflection, being an inexperienced 20-year-old, I was attempting to deal with a situation for which I had had no training. I realised I was learning the hard way, when suddenly the Naval Officer I mentioned earlier appeared. Blasting away at the top of his voice he lashed out his arms to the left and then the right. Even the sight of this giant, with gold braid on his uniform sleeve and bearing the clear stamp of authority, did little to calm the panic from taking hold. At last he stood back, drew his .45 revolver and held it above his head. "I'll shoot the next man who panics," he roared. While some looked at him in disbelief, others simply ignored him and continued pressing forward. He levelled his revolver at a group who were fighting amongst themselves and fired. Part of the top of one man's head crumpled and there was a spattering of blood all around. "Who's next?" he bellowed. Like magic, all calmed down and stared at him in a stunned silence. He kicked the body of the man he had killed into the surf and then strode furiously around lining up the now docile troops.

When the boat had re-loaded, the Officer moving back to the beach caught sight of me. He looked into my eyes and said, "That's all you have to do Sergeant to stop a panic." I believed him and realised that this was a situation he had no doubt been faced with before. Strangely enough, I was not horrified. I was experiencing traumatic events earlier in my life than many men of my age or older would ever see. I knew it would help me in the future to face up to similar situations, should they occur, but I didn't expect them to be like the one I was now experiencing. The last two horrifying hours had inured me to being caught up in a desperate struggle for survival.

Some time later the Naval Officer approached where I was standing, together with three more Sergeants, and said to us, "Follow me." We went to a hollow in the sand dunes where we were given mugs of hot soup. "Look at that shower," he said pointing towards the beach, "No discipline, too many part-timers. When this is over, if we ever get back to England, all of us will know that our salvation will be due to a handful of real professional soldiers on the perimeter. Hear them now."

We could hear the noise of the battle in the distance and I thought to myself, "Those brave soldiers should be given a medal." The Germans had a system whereby they awarded special metal clasps to those who had been involved in, for instance, hand-to-hand fighting. Our country offers no such acknowledgement.

After spending a short period on the beach we seemed to have developed a sense of extreme fatalism. Here we were, large groups of men digging below ground level, some with bare hands, the more fortunate with entrenching tools. Everyone had realised after a number of air attacks, that our hold on life was tenuous in the extreme. During the air raids, the noise was absolutely deafening, and the blast from bombs falling nearby sometimes rolled us over and over. The cries of the wounded immediately after these raids were unforgettable.

Only a few rescue ships appeared to be arriving and those that did were lucky to remain afloat. There was a feeling of anguish that our predicament was becoming hopeless. More of the Stuka air attacks, which seemed to arrive without a pause, would leave bomb craters on every square yard of the beach. We had now become acutely familiar with the urgent cries of "stretcher bearer." It had become a hollow cry. Even the stretcher-bearers were either among the wounded, or by then completely exhausted.

Since 10th May, the Germans' real terror weapon had been the Stuka dive-bomber. During the retreat to the coast the sky had been full of them. We appeared to be their sole target. We would hear the drone of their engines getting nearer, then the high pitched screech of the plane diving on to its target, followed by the blast of the bomb itself. We thought we could not possibly survive these seemingly endless attacks, but we did. During one raid, a stick of bombs dropped very close to where we were, throwing bodies in the air. One of them landed near to me. It was a young soldier who slowly opened his eyes, holding his hand out to me, which I grasped. As he held my hand tightly I noticed that he had been hit in his chest by a jagged piece of shrapnel. He was breathing with a rasping, wheezing sound, as blood began to bubble up out of his chest. I said to him, "I'll get my field dressing out." He replied, "Don't bother, no chance." For about a minute he gripped my hand tighter and tighter, then the grip loosened, and he was gone. It seemed to me that he had gripped my hand, a complete stranger, as his last contact in this world.

After the mishaps during the beach loading earlier in the day, we were taking a well-earned rest in our favourite hollow in the dunes. We could hear the sound of small arms firing coming from the general direction of the canal, which we had crossed to get to the beach. It was evident that the Germans had made a small infantry crossing, which turned out to be only a minor penetration. A small armoured reconnaissance vehicle had crossed the bridge only to find that it had been blown up behind them.

Suddenly, our Officer popped up from the sand dunes and ordered, "Follow me." This did not appear to be a very attractive proposition as we began to move together with another group in the direction of the German vehicle. Our firing on the 'recce' was so strong, however, that its three-man crew baled out, but we decided not to take them prisoners. On checking the War Diary from our 9th Army Field Workshop Unit, the entry read 'One German tank captured and as this seems to have been a lone scout the defenders withdrew.' I believe this could be described as the fog of war.

I then joined an odd collection of all arms of the service. We began to move along the sea front as there appeared to be no movement on the section of beach where we were. The heavy air bombardment and the sinking of so many ships had caused a temporary pause in the evacuation. Having lost contact with my unit, I became friends with a guardsman, a regular soldier who seemed to be taking the whole situation in his stride. We met an Officer who was evidently following instructions by advising everyone to move from La Panne along the front of the coast towards the harbour of Dunkirk, about five or six miles distant.

Huge black clouds of smoke could be seen drifting upward from burning oil tanks, and as we got closer to the outskirts of Dunkirk we passed piles of bodies with British Army boots, sticking out from the lorry tarpaulins which covered them.

A battery of 40mm guns was still firing at attacking aircraft as we reached a row of terraced houses. We entered them looking for food and water, but most of the houses had already been broken into.

Eventually reaching a house which was still intact, we smashed a window with our rifle butts and clambered in. There were tins of food and bottles of white wine in the pantry. After refreshing ourselves we moved on. Daylight was fading as we joined a file of men moving along the sea front and reaching a point where there appeared to be some semblance of order. It was now dark and I could make out a Naval Officer holding a megaphone ordering groups to make their way to the Mole. As we got closer, an Embarkation Officer was calmly shouting, "Come on boys, don't take any notice of those horrid Germans. All aboard the Skylark, back in time for tea." Nearby, a soldier was kneeling with his hands folded as in prayer. He said, "For the last few miles I have been praying for the British Navy and here they are." It was now 2.00 a.m. and quite dark. Darkness meant that we did not have to suffer any further air attacks.

We filed in line along the Mole, at one point having to balance ourselves, gripping a rope beside a narrow plank, which was bridging a gap where a heavy bomb had demolished part of the Mole. We then had to climb down a ladder and step onto a small fishing vessel. There was an overwhelming smell of engine oil and sweaty bodies. We clambered aboard the boat and stood up. We were so cramped that when I wanted to blow my nose I could not reach down to get my handkerchief. It was a great relief when the boat began to chug away and I tried to turn my head around and look back at the red and orange skyline. The terrible sight I saw made me realise that I was lucky to have got away. At that moment my thoughts were of those men still fighting and holding the line in the rearguard. Their only chance to get away from Dunkirk would be at nightfall.

We could see the odd winking light ahead of us where a channel had been swept of mines. We were thankful for this until we heard the familiar drone of aircraft above us, then a big splash rocked the boat. A voice rang out, "What's that Skipper?" The reply came in a broad southern accent, "It's only a magnetic mine." "What's a magnetic mine?" "That's okay son, don't worry, this is a wooden boat." The British sense of humour, which was bantered around, was a wonderful fillip in keeping our spirits up.

The sea was calm and we, standing packed tightly together and lulled by the rocking of the boat, drifted off to sleep for the first time in days. We were awakened by a great roar. Looking to the front, about a mile ahead, was the boat, which had left Dunkirk before us. It was on fire. As we got nearer we could see men struggling in the water. We could see a Royal Naval Corvette picking up survivors. Suddenly, there was a grating noise and a violent rocking of our boat. We had collided with and glanced off the naval vessel. Having awoken suddenly after a long period of sleeping standing up, two men on the edge of the boat and in a confused state, jumped overboard. Watching them struggling in the water by the light of a hand lamp directed from the naval vessel, a voice boomed out, "Keep moving, we'll pick them up." I thought that at least there was now room to get my hand into my pocket and get my handkerchief out.

As we sailed into the darkness and to England, I began to recall the horrible sights I had seen from the beach. I had watched a German Stuka attack a British destroyer, which had picked up hundreds of troops. They could be seen packed tightly on the deck, their faces upturned to the diving planes, then disappearing as they dropped on to the deck. A direct hit on the destroyer brought a great flash and clouds of steam and smoke, which as it cleared revealed the boat, which appeared to be keeling over with survivors of the raid jumping overboard and into the water. That was not the end of it, as in came a further attack and there were yet more casualties. Bodies could be seen floating in the sea, while the men who had survived were clinging desperately to floating debris.

Dawn was breaking when the most beautiful sight we had ever seen came into view – the English coastline! A rousing cheer echoed around the boat. The skipper commented, "That's how the last lot reacted." We then realised that this old fisherman had risked his life and his boat to save us, and others before us, and was possibly going to make another dangerous trip at nightfall. He was one of the many unsung heroes, to whom we owed a great debt.

It was with a heartfelt feeling of relief among her motley passengers that our boat nosed its way into Margate Harbour. Approaching the jetty we could see a crowd of people looking down at us. They broke into spontaneous cheering. While we thought we had taken part in an enormous defeat, we were being greeted as if we had been victorious. Scrambling up a ladder and onto the jetty, an officer cadet approached me and said, "Follow me Sergeant to the Railway Station, I will carry your rifle." I replied, "I've carried this a long way and I'm not going to let go of it until I hand it over officially. Thanks all the same."

As we were shepherded onto a train, welcome mugs of tea and large door-stopper portions of bread and cheese were handed to us to be eaten ravenously. We had survived the horrors of Dunkirk. As I sat on the train I reflected on the old saying, "He who fights and runs away, lives to fight another day." Little did I realise that within two years I would be taking part in another defeat – The Fall of Tobruk.

The special train we travelled on was full of Dunkirk survivors. Slowly passing through stations on our way north, we saw groups of civilians standing on the platforms cheering us wildly, bringing lumps to battle-hardened, but weary, soldiers' throats. I looked around trying to locate any of my old comrades who had arrived with me on the beach. I could see no one. Dunkirk had become a veritable melting pot.

Our destination turned out to be Nottingham. On arrival we eagerly handed in the sea-soaked and smelly uniforms in which we had lived, worked, fought and slept in for many days. We were given the luxury of a hot bath, then shaved off the emergence of a beard. I then received a magic piece of paper – my Travel Document, a 48-hour leave pass. Then followed a train journey from Nottingham to my home in Sheffield.

Back home, on a full stomach after eating a meal of my mother's superb cooking, I felt, at last, at peace with the world, even though it was a deeply troubled one. As I sat with my parents round the table I was bemused by the absolute confidence they had as to what lay ahead. I did not explain to them that all we, the British Armed Forces, had to defend ourselves with against a far superior, well-equipped and highly trained German Army and Air Force, were one rifle and five rounds of ammunition per man. I knew that should the Germans defeat the heavily depleted Royal Navy then we did not have a 'cat in hell's chance' of winning the war. I consoled myself with the thought that it was through this supreme confidence that the mighty British Empire had been built.

Back In The U.K., The Blitz

After the leave I returned to my unit. We reassembled at Rhyl in North Wales and were allocated to Coastal Defence. It seemed to be a misnomer that we should be defending the West Coast, an area which was the least likely to be attacked, but bear in mind our heavy armament – one rifle plus five rounds of ammunition per man.

In the re-organisation I was posted to a staff job at Western Command Headquarters based in Chester, where I was given the impressive title of: P.A. to D.A.D.O.S(E). Otherwise – Personal Assistant to the Deputy Assistant Director of Ordnance Services (Engineering). For this very important position I received no extra pay! My Colonel was in charge of numerous matters, one of them being responsible for all the Ack Ack guns covering an area from Liverpool to Cardiff and westwards to Coventry.

Fig: 6. June 1940. The author (aged 20) is on the left of this photograph, which was taken soon after his escape from Dunkirk. The sergeant on the motorcycle volunteered to cover the retreat of his comrades, including the author, with a 'Boyes' anti-tank rifle. He held out until he disabled oncoming reconnaissance vehicles, thus blocking the road, then made good his own escape on a motorcycle.

From September 1940, almost every night a British city was being heavily bombed by the German Luftwaffe. These raids were referred to by us as 'Blitzes'. One of the first was a massive raid on Coventry. On the morning following that raid our phone rang and it was the Gunnery Officer in charge of the Anti Aircraft guns in the Coventry area. They had fired so constantly during the raid of the previous night, he reported, that the liners of their gun barrels were now so worn that they were inaccurate and useless. He requested replacement liners for his guns. Our Colonel told him, "We have no spare liners." The reply from the Gunnery Officer was, "What shall I do?" The Colonel told him to, "Keep the guns firing, it will keep the bloody civilians happy".

Fig: 7. Coventry Cathedral, following the devastating air raid on the night of November 14th 1940. This raid was the first by the Luftwaffe where they used radio beams to guide the attacking aircraft onto their target.

The following day, having a few hours off duty, I was taking a walk in the lovely countryside that surrounds Chester. The peaceful atmosphere was disturbed by the sound of an approaching aircraft. Due to heavy cloud cover I could not see the plane or identify it. There was a sudden rattle of machine gunfire and a screeching noise as a German bomber, already in flames, appeared through the cloud hurtling to the ground, crashing with an ear-shattering explosion a short distance away from me. In the evening I was in the Black Swan pub in Chester, when a number of R.A.F. personnel came into the place to be treated to an evening's free drinking at the expense of the local residents.

Having previously experienced the horrors of the war, the activity and the comradeship that had existed, and now finding myself in a staff position at Western Command H.Q., I soon became extremely bored. I determined to get away and got myself transferred on to a Physical Training course. Once I had completed the course and qualified as an Assistant Physical Training Instructor, I was posted to a Workshop Unit close to Manchester's Trafford Docks. My duties there were to organise evening keep-fit classes for the Home Guard. As I watched these well meaning, but grossly unfit civilian Home Guard volunteers trying to cope with the unarmed combat procedures, I could not help but ponder on how they would fare against well trained German forces should the occasion ever arise.

I was then moved to an Army Barracks on the Upper Chorlton Road, a thoroughfare that led directly into the centre of Manchester. Part of our duties was the support of the civilian emergency services in coping with the results of German air attacks on the city that at that time were being made almost nightly. The local Auxiliary Fire Service would turn out, moving at a high speed to the fires and we would follow on behind to assist in the clearing of debris and the rescuing of people trapped in the wreckage of bombed buildings. We also assisted the Bomb Disposal Units, but were kept at a safe distance, mainly to prevent onlookers getting into the danger zone.

During one raid the Bomb Disposal Unit located an unexploded bomb, which had bounced off a building. They had checked the fuse, which fortunately was not ticking, loaded it on to a cradle on their truck, then brought the bomb into an area in front of our Barracks. Although members of the unit advised us that it was safe, it looked very spectacular there, with flags fluttering from each corner marked U.X.B. *(Un-Exploded Bomb)*

As we drank mugs of tea, the C.O. pointed to the houses across the road from the Barracks. Their curtains could be seen being pulled slightly back. He remarked, "We shall certainly be invited by them for tea and cakes. Let's hope they have some attractive daughters." The bomb was later removed to a safe area for detonation.

Liverpool To Egypt. The Long Way Round

In early November we received orders to prepare to be sent overseas, and in preparation for this we were moved to a building near Liverpool, where we were issued with tropical kit, which meant we were bound for the Middle or Far East. On a miserable rainy day we got off a train at a station close to Liverpool Docks, straight into the aftermath of a heavy German air raid, which had taken place during the night. We struggled across streets littered with rubble and, burdened with our heavy and cumbersome kit, we had a real taste of army travel. The last lap towards the troopship we were about to board was a scramble over enormous piles of tins of Heinz beans, which had been blown out from a dockside storage warehouse after a direct hit.

We were very impressed when we saw the R.M.S. "Orduna". The boat had been owned by the Pacific Steam Navigation Company line and had, in happier times, been a passenger liner cruising regularly to India. Boarding it, we were pleasantly surprised to see it had not yet been converted for troop carrying. All ranks of Staff Sergeant and above were allocated comfortable double bunked cabins. We sailed up the Irish Sea, hugging the Scottish Western Isles. Strong gales sprang up. Each morning the breakfast of bacon and eggs became ever less well attended as the weather worsened. Those with iron stomachs, and fortunately I was one, were served with double helpings.

When the convoy was fully assembled it was huge, containing many thousands of troops and huge quantities of equipment and stores. Our convoy also had the protection of a large fleet of escort vessels. We sailed north until we were near the Arctic Circle, then the convoy made a huge sweeping turn, on to a heading of due south. Having always carried a compass, I found it fascinating plotting the course we were taking. At that time, German submarines were limited in their range and unable to raid as widely across the Atlantic as they would do in later years and so we were able to keep clear of them.

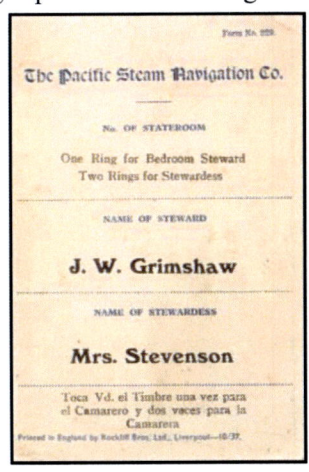

Fig: 8. The RMS Orduna was still operating on a peacetime basis when we sailed. We were well taken care of by Mr Grimshaw and Mrs Stevenson.

We continued to sail down the middle of the North Atlantic and eventually refuelling at Sierra Leone in West Africa. The heat was now sweltering, but we were treated to the fascinating sight of dolphins and flying fish leaping through the waves ahead of and alongside our ship. While we were lying at anchor and refuelling in Sierra Leone, we amused ourselves by throwing coins overboard and watching young native boys diving to recover them.

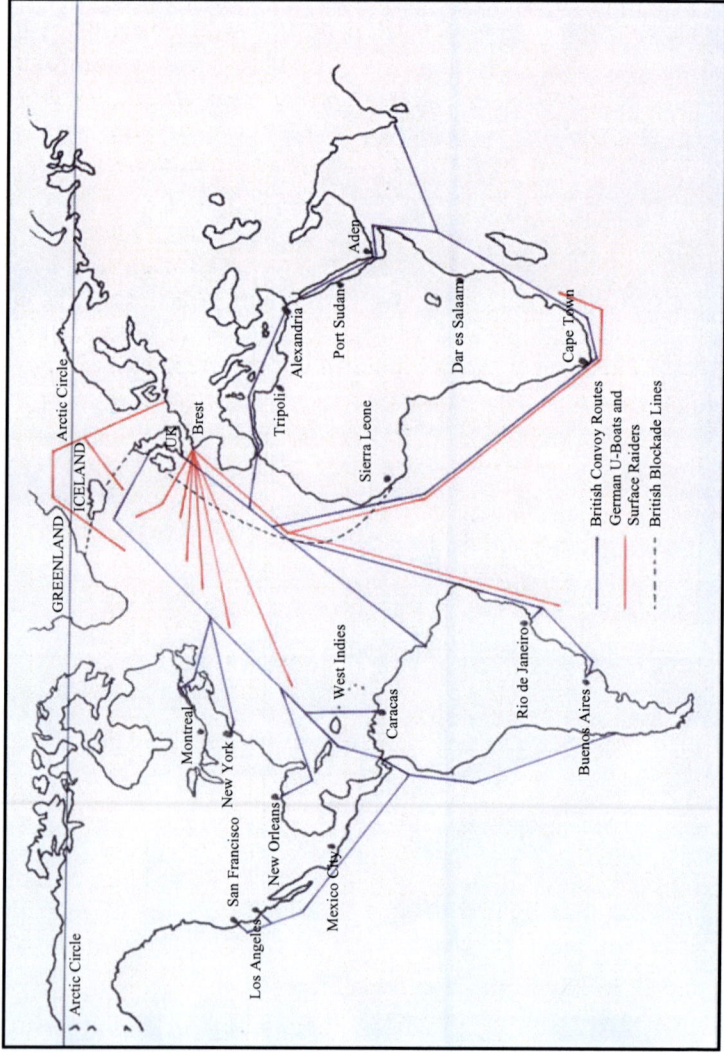

Fig: 9. The major convoy routes and Axis submarine and surface raider patrolled areas. The author's route via Sierra Leone and the Cape of Good Hope is clearly shown.

Resuming our journey, we sailed southwards towards the Cape of Good Hope where we passed close to schools of large whales blowing spray. Rounding the Cape, we were amongst huge swells at the junction of the South Atlantic and the Indian Ocean. We were given a few days leave in Durban until New Year's Day, then it was back on board. The convoy sailed north to Aden and then through the Red Sea, which is over a thousand miles long. And all this in wartime and a comfortable cabin!

I enjoyed every minute and mile of that journey, several times being allowed to take turns on watch, standing on the bridge, wearing a large duffel coat, as the boat sailed through the bitterly cold North Atlantic, where the rigging became completely covered with icicles. When we reached equatorial regions, we changed into our tropical kit. We finally arrived at Kantara, the Egyptian port at the southern end of the Suez Canal, where we finally disembarked from our 'cruise'. We spent a short time here being instructed on Middle East hygiene, which is non-existent among the local inhabitants. We then had a stern lecture by a tough, long serving Sergeant Major on how to cope in a primitive country where thieving is the norm. It was not long before we had personal experience of this. In spite of doubling the guards at night, some Arab thieves crept silently into the camp, jacked up a lorry and stole all the wheels. The explosive comments from the Sergeant Major the following morning – which cannot be written here – made us all feel very small, but he had made his point.

To Palestine

We moved forward along the single-track railway leading north towards Palestine to relieve a unit doing a spell of duty guarding a huge stores dump at Gaza in the Negev Desert. It was not to be an easy task. We noticed on travelling up this railway from Egypt many groups of wild looking Bedouin tribesmen.

Arriving fresh from England, we received friendly taunts from the old hands of "Get your knees brown." The Depot Adjutant inspected us, giving the usual lecture on how to conduct ourselves in the Middle East. He told us we were to spend a few weeks getting acclimatised. "These Wogs," he said, "who live around here labouring for us are not the desert Sheiks you may have seen in 'The Desert Song'. They are a set of low down thieving bastards, who would stick a knife in your back to pinch your breath if there was any value in it. When on night duty you will move around in pairs, and if anything moves you will shoot it. I mean that and those are my orders." I thought this was the most direct order I had ever been given.

A few nights later I took my first patrol out to check the far flank of the depot. Passing the huge sheet covered dump, I detected a group of shadowy figures together with a camel moving off quickly. I shouted, "Halt." We did what many an old army veteran would have done. 'Shoved one up the spout'. "Shall we fire?" came from one of my men. I replied, "Yes." Although I had one of the intruders in my rifle sights, I hesitated to shoot. I had come out to shoot Germans and Italians, and not unarmed civilians. Our shots went wide and the thieves escaped. The next day we were ordered on to the Rifle Range for shooting practice.

The following night another Sergeant on patrol shot and killed an Arab thief. He was immediately promoted to Staff Sergeant. The dead body was laid out at the entrance to the Depot. When the local Sheik riding his donkey arrived leading his workers, a loud wail to 'Allah' went up from them. The Adjutant stood by the body, shouting loudly at them in Arabic and warning that any other thieves who tried to steal our property would be shot. It was then that I realised I had entered a different world.

After the shooting incident, there were loud protests and much grumbling among the Arab labourers, because they thought they deserved a higher rate of pay. The inevitable trouble finally erupted the morning I was Guard Commander. The guard hut was sited close to the Main Entrance of the depot through which the workers trooped just after dawn each morning. Our orders were to turn out half a dozen guards on the gate as the Arabs, normally about 200, slouched past. On this particular morning I looked through the guard hut window and, on seeing in the distance a cloud of dust heralding the approach of our labourers, alerted the guard. Walking into the hut the Officer of the Guard, who had begun his career as a regular soldier and had been promoted up through the ranks, appeared. He was as tough as nails and spoke fluent Arabic. Looking through the window at the approaching mass, he said, "There's something afoot." The cloud of dust approaching now appeared more intense than on other mornings, a noise resembling a thousand angry bees could be heard, punctuated with shouting and screaming. They were picking up stones and flinging them in front, raising clouds of sand. Leading the crowd was the local Sheik, an evil looking character, grossly overweight and balancing on a small donkey. The nearer they came, the more ugly the situation looked.

"Phone through and turn out a full guard," the Officer said quietly, "and get your men to cover me when I go and deal with this rabble." He took a long rawhide whip down from the wall. The rest of the guard had by this time arrived and were duly lined up across the main entrance to our camp. The Officer took up position in front of the guard and gave his instructions. "Don't shoot until I give you the order, and then make it five rounds over their heads." He then strode forward, a lone impressive figure with his whip in his hand, flexing it from side to side. This man was in complete command of the situation, advancing single handed on a wild mob of Arabs. Suddenly he broke into a sprint cracking the whip over his head and roaring at the top of his voice in Arabic. The shower of stones which had been flying all around him, gradually diminished and the mob came to a halt, staring at the Officer as if mesmerised. For a few seconds the Sheik paused nervously, then turned tail and fled, the rest of the mob rapidly following on behind him. What had threatened to become an ugly situation was now under control.

The Officer hurled a last torrent of abuse at the retreating Arabs and then strode back to join us. He wiped the sweat from his brow and handed me the whip. "Hang it back on the wall and if they come again and I'm not around, that is all you have to do." Have you done that before?" I said to him. "Not here," he replied, "but many times before I've been in a similar situation where quick strong action won the day. After all, that is what I've been trained for. Discipline wins the day and you, no doubt just out from dear old England, think that I'm a crude old bugger. Out here this is a rough, crude life and if you do not conform to that you won't survive." To me, his advice was important.

It was not long after the above events, that we found ourselves in Palestine. It was a great change from Egypt, here the Jewish population had cultivated as much of their land as possible and the fields were a deep luscious green. The exception to this rule was the area around Jaffa, which was an Arab town. We were stationed outside Haifa. The Jews were not over friendly towards the British troops, seeing us as a pro-Arab occupying force. I tried unsuccessfully to make friends with a Jewish family. In the evenings I visited a local Armenian bar, in preference to the N.A.A.F.I. Here I met an Arab named Saieed who spoke good English. We became very good friends and from him I learned of the complicated politics of that particular part of the world, albeit from an Arab point of view. (Many years later, as an Export Manager, I had the opportunity to visit Israel regularly on business. I made many friends, but also learned that the Arab/Jewish problem appeared to be insoluble, due to the intolerant religious demands of both nations).

Fig: 10. In Palestine during 1941. Honing my musical skills.

And So To The Western Desert

My relationship with the Jews became closer after I left Haifa, moving out to the Western Desert in charge of a detachment of Jewish volunteers who were being drafted there as reinforcements. On our long journey by rail across the Negev, then through the Egyptian Delta, I got to know these men better and was interested to learn that, before volunteering, they had been doctors, dentists and university professors. They were the most remarkable soldiers I had ever met. They had joined the British Army as auxiliaries in Palestine, having fled from Europe, where largely as a result of Nazi domination, Anti-Semitism was the rule rather than the exception.

While travelling through Egypt, we stopped overnight at a place called Zag-a-Zig. For recreation that evening, the Movements Officer suggested what he described as the local 'Gin Palace'. Together with three other Sergeants, I made my way to what we quickly found to be nothing more than a 'drinking den', where the only refreshment available was beer.

Fig: 11. The author is on the far right in this photograph, taken in the Nile Delta en route to the Western Desert in 1942.

Inside were round marble-topped tables on cast iron legs. We ordered our beers and looked around. The place was full of British troops, both on the ground floor and on a balcony above.

To understand what happened next, it is necessary to understand a little of the history of the desert war.

During the first British offensive under the command of General Wavell, the 7th Armoured Division carried all before them up to a line near Agedabia. By the time they got there, both tanks and vehicles were in a sorry state after an advance of several hundred miles. So, the 7th Armoured were pulled back to Egypt to rest and refit and were replaced by the 1st Armoured Division, newly arrived and not yet acclimatised to desert conditions. No sooner had they arrived than Rommel attacked with full force, causing the 1st Armoured to retreat with all speed and swiftly lose all the gains made by the 7th.

To say there was a certain amount of 'needle' between the two divisions would be to put it mildly.

Soon, the ribald banter between the 7th on the ground floor and the 1st on the balcony became rather 'pointed', which led to a bottle being hurled from the balcony and landing on a table, where it shattered in a shower of blood and glass. From there the situation rapidly 'developed', to the point where, amidst a fusillade of bottles, my colleagues and myself made our way towards the exit by dragging our table with us as a mobile shelter.

We just about made it to the exit as someone fired the first shot from his .38 pistol into the ceiling, from where it ricocheted round the room. As return fire was delivered we made good our escape and vanished into the gloom just as the convoy of Military Police vehicles arrived.

If anyone talks to me about being involved in a roughhouse, I always think back to that night and smile knowingly!

During the long and arduous trip we talked a great deal and I found it interesting during the evenings sitting around and listening to tales of their lives in Germany, Hungary and Yugoslavia etc., and of how they had made their way to Palestine, only to become further disillusioned at not being able to find work. In our conversations, I pointed out some of the more salient facets of military life and how tough they would find their lives to be in the Western Desert. I suggested that they keep together as a group, if only to preserve the quality of discussion and conversation they generated, for the British soldier is not noted for his wide-ranging and intellectually stimulating conversation.

The Western Desert fascinated me. There was a strong sense of adventure about being able to find one's way in the limitless stretches of sand and stony wastes. It was completely different from anything I had experienced before. From the moment I got off the train at Mersa Matruh, I instinctively felt this was the place for me. All the way on the rail journey up from the Delta, I had sat at the open door of the railway truck gazing at the ever-changing scenery. I watched the lush green field of the Delta slowly change to the stark beauty of the desert, then a landscape of rough camel scrub and finally the real shifting sandy desert. Wave after wave of sand as far as the eye could see, shimmering in the heat of the day, ethereal by night, especially when a limpid moon hung in the star patterned sky. I had never seen stars as bright. I was excited to learn that later I would be instructed in how to find my way by these stars.

Fig: 12. The author (aged 21), at Sidi Rezagh, in the Western Desert 1942.

Later, when I was in my dug-out at Tobruk, looking up at a moonless sky before dropping off to sleep, I would watch the stars move slowly across the sky. By then I was able to pick out the various constellations gaining both a sense of pleasure and detachment from the arduous situation I was in.

Having arrived at Mersa Matruh, I reported to the Movement Officer with the Jewish draft I had brought with me from Palestine. The journey had been a long one, all the way from Haifa, via Gaza, then through the Sinai Desert, across the Suez Canal, traversing Egypt, and to the Libyan border.

I was regarded by the men I was in charge of as something of a 'nut case', because I would go off for a stroll on my own in the desert. This was because the vast majority of troops I met regarded the desert as a hostile environment. They had not had the training required to prepare them properly for the tough life they were all about to experience in the very near future.

Fig: 13. 'Brewing up' at the railhead, Mersa Matruh 1942, while en route to Tobruk.

The following day my group and I piled into trucks and set off along a sandy track, heading for Tobruk. After having travelled for two hours the convoy stopped for a 'brew up'. I was to be initiated into the brewing of desert tea. Hanging on the back of every 8th Army vehicle was the 'brew can'. As water was severely rationed this was the best way of slaking a thirst. A hole was scooped out of the sand, doused with petrol, and the brew can placed in the hole. Standing well away, a match would be thrown into the hole and the water soon boiled. This was before the era of tea bags and a large measure of tea-leaves were poured into the water which gave it a thick brown consistency that almost made it possible for the teaspoon to stand up straight in it. As the water had been kept in lightweight metal water cans it had to be doped with chlorine tablets, and this is what made the tea so strong. The bitter taste had to be disguised, usually with two teaspoons of sugar and a teaspoon of condensed milk. Convoy regulations stated there had to be a ten-minute tea break every two hours. After driving for two hours surrounded by swirling dust and hot sand, we realised why these regular stops were so essential.

After our 'tea break' we were on the move again. Half an hour later the desert bared its teeth, when a cloud no bigger than my hand appeared. The leading vehicle pulled to a stop and the rest of the convoy closed up to it nose to tail. The R.A.S.C. Sergeant in charge came down the line and spoke to the men in each truck. "Any of you lads ever been in a Khamseen before?" "No, what's a Khamseen?" "Bloody great sandstorm, the likes of which you have never seen before. It blots the whole landscape out. Regulations are that you stop when you see it coming, take a bearing on the track ahead as it will all soon be wiped out. When the Khamseen blows itself out, there will be no track ahead. Don't forget there are no roads in this part of the world. Have you got a scarf?" A scarf with a uniform! "Didn't anyone tell you that a scarf is an absolutely vital item in the desert as it keeps the sand out of your mouth and eyes." "No one told us about that before we left Base." "As usual those ignorant Base Wallahs know nothing about the desert. You have to learn the hard way."

Climbing back into the cab, I watched both fascinated and amazed as the dark brown wall of sand came hurtling towards us. Suddenly, it lashed into the truck, which lurched violently, I then realised the power of it. The noise was deafening as myriads of sharp particles of sand hit the windscreen. We had our sand goggles tightly on and I stuffed my scarf around my face and neck. I was the only one with a scarf. Although the Khamseen lasted only a few minutes, it gave us a lesson to be prepared in the future.

Fig:14. Messerschmitt BF109 fighter in desert trim. These aircraft were used for hit-and-run raids on Allied troops and transport throughout the German-led desert campaigns.

Fig: 15. The Heinkel He111 bomber was used extensively by the Luftwaffe during the desert war in many roles, including ground strafing from the nose and underbelly gun positions.

Forward To Tobruk

After having served in the desert for a few months we had become experienced in how, if caught out in the open, to cope with sand storms, which occurred frequently at certain times of the year. We would crouch down with our backs to the onslaught or look for a slit trench, which offered the best form of protection. After a sandstorm had moved away, we would strip off all our clothes, even our underwear, shaking off the sand. Looking along the trucks we were travelling in, we would normally find that they had completely disappeared. We also had to keep a close watch on the empty oil drums that had been weighted down with stones. These were the markers for the tracks on which we had to drive.

Our route eventually took us to Sidi Barrani and Sollum where we crossed the wire separating Egypt from Libya and stopped the night in a wadi, west of Bardia. In one of the earlier campaigns in the Western Desert, a small British Army under the command of General Wavell defeated a large Italian force in this area. At that time the Italians would regularly fire a long-range gun at our defences. The gun was christened 'Bardia Bill'. While stopping at Bardia for a tea break, an Officer with the detachment there said that if we stopped the night en route we could 'kip' down in a suitable wadi, at the same time warning me that we were to be on alert for attacks by enemy aircraft. They usually came inland from the sea, especially on moonlit nights, spraying machine gun fire indiscriminately at any reinforcements making their way in the direction of Tobruk.

That night the moon was full and brilliant. I went round checking on my Palestinian charges and, as they were bedding down, I told them to erect a stone barrier to give them protection against any air attacks. They seemed to me to be old men – in their late 30s or over – and I was only 23. I felt as if I was an experienced old soldier.

I told them to move away from the trucks, which could be visible as targets to attacking aircraft. Although they were tired and grumbling, they saw sense in my advice. We eventually wrapped our blankets around us, tried to get as comfortable as possible, and dropped off to sleep. We were suddenly awakened by shouts of "Take cover." Looking up we saw a string of 'candelabra' flares lighting up the area. A number of fighter planes came roaring in over our heads sending out streams of tracer bullets, which were ricocheting off the surrounding rocks with a tremendous clatter. It was all over in a few minutes. I went to check if we had any casualties, and fortunately every one of the men was unhurt. The R.A.S.C. Sergeant drily observed that the Germans never seemed to actually hit anything, they only did it to frighten the new arrivals.

On the move again the next morning, we passed through El Adem. Once more I found that all those romantic Middle Eastern names were just a few shattered buildings surrounded by camouflaged tents. Bumping along the rutted bomb-damaged track we breasted a rise in the escarpment, and there below was Tobruk. This was the largest settlement we had been to since the Delta. Shimmering in the heat, a collection of white buildings, many without roofs, were clustered around the harbour, flanked by the deep blue of the Mediterranean Sea. Since leaving Haifa we had travelled about 1,200 miles to get to Tobruk.

We drove down the track, stopping briefly at a large military cemetery containing hundreds of rough graves of soldiers who had been killed in the previous siege. Our driver, an old 'Desert Rat', pointed out to us several graves of V.C.s and other highly decorated heroes. "Plenty of spaces have been left for you lot when the next siege starts," he drily commented. Down by the harbour, we pulled up outside the Town Major's Office.

I went in from the stifling outside heat to the relatively cool inside atmosphere and handed my Movement Order to the Adjutant. While he was checking the details the unmistakable drone of approaching enemy aircraft could be heard. I glanced nervously around the room expecting to see that everyone had made for the numerous slit trenches outside. No one had moved. They appeared to be unperturbed as the noise grew louder. The Adjutant looked up, "Don't worry old chap, this happens all the time. When you have been here a few days you will be able to distinguish the engine tone of both German and Italian bombers. The Italians fly so high we ignore them but when the Dorniers come over then we take cover." A little later great plumes of spray could be seen rising out of the water where the bombs had dropped. I learned later that the Italians didn't care for flying along the coastline, as this would put them in reach of our 3.7inch guns. They would approach from the sea, dropping their bomb loads short of the target before turning tail. As we left, the Adjutant reminded us, "Don't forget that if they are Germans then take cover."

My unit was stationed about a couple of miles outside Tobruk in the direction of Gazala. We were relatively comfortable at this distance, having a grandstand view of the daily bombing of the harbour. It was fascinating to watch the silver bombs showering down. One of our cockney lads ran a book on whether there would be any direct hits on the shipping.

Just before the real battle commenced in May, the Germans concentrated their bombing mainly on the shipping. The whole area of the harbour would disappear from sight in great clouds of water, spray, dust and smoke. During one raid, a naval destroyer was hit and keeled over in an awesome display of exploding ammunition. I shuddered to think of the fate of the ship's stokers trapped below decks, surrounded by exploding ammunition and bursting boilers.

Early one morning as the sun was rising over the horizon I watched the N.A.A.F.I. wagon wending its way towards us, bringing our weekly ration of 50 cigarettes and one bottle of beer each. An early morning German Heinkel appeared, flying in low and quietly towards our escarpment and coming up behind the N.A.A.F.I. wagon. He machine-gunned and destroyed it, together with the driver and our rations. Later that day we were reflecting on the happenings of the day, particularly the loss of our 'cigs and booze'. One of the lads commented, "It was all the driver's fault. He should have kept his bloody eyes open." I agreed with him, realising that in so short a space of time, I had, like my comrades, become hardened to the constant presence of violent death and destruction and able to cope with what was happening around me.

Later, in civilian life when faced with problems, I would look around and see colleagues with worried looks on their faces. I would then cast my mind back to my service days, realising the problem I now faced was by comparison small to the point of insignificance. Today when disasters occur and people rush to see counsellors, I often wonder on what basis of harsh experience Counsellors base the advice they give to those who come to them.

I took a 'recce' party out to inspect an abandoned Italian Army stores dump. There were piles of war material lying around. Rifles, uniforms, pith helmets, shell cases, and many other items hastily discarded by an army in retreat. I had been given strict instructions to beware of 'booby' traps. We came to an area where a number of brightly coloured metal objects painted half red and half blue, about the size of a Mills Bomb, were lying on the ground. Against the brown sand they stood out in contrast. I called to the Sergeant Armourer saying, "What the devil are these?"

Taking a look at them he said, "The Italians leave these things around in the hope that some daft buggers will be fascinated by them and pick them up. They have a sensitive detonating device and will explode on touch." I quickly warned everyone with me not to touch them. They would have to be removed by a Bomb Disposal Team.

That evening just as the sun was setting, I had 'enjoyed' my usual luxurious meal of bully beef and biscuits and was relaxing in the dugout, smoking my Bruno-filled pipe when there was a sudden sharp crack and a scream from the direction of the Italian dump. Rushing forward, I saw Private Nelson staggering towards me with blood dripping from his hand. I had always thought the only duty suitable for him was that of Latrine Wallah. "What's happened?" I shouted. "I've lost some fingers," he moaned. He held up his right hand and I saw that several fingers were missing and the palm of his hand was a raw mess. I got out a field dressing and stemmed the flow of blood. He appeared to be bemused and oblivious to the pain. "What happened?" I asked him, although I had already guessed. "It's them red and blue things," he said. "I kept looking at them all day and I couldn't take my eyes off 'em. I know you said I shouldn't touch 'em but I couldn't resist it, so I went over and picked one up." I wouldn't have believed it possible after my firm warnings to all the men, but if it was going to happen, it could only have happened to Private Nelson. The Italians must have realised that some British soldiers were as thick as two short planks and they had at least been successful in putting one of our men permanently out of the war.

Another instance of a British soldier being stupid beyond belief came a few weeks later, when I took out a patrol in search of a truck which had gone missing in the desert. The driver of the truck and an armourer had gone to a certain map reference south of our camp to service a Hussar Regiment tank which had developed a turret problem. The squadron had moved off without the turret being repaired, but had wirelessed their new position and reported that the armourer had not arrived the previous day as expected. As we were able to follow their tracks, we had been searching for several hours when suddenly we saw the whirling mass of a Khamseen approaching us. We stopped and sheltered against the back of our wagon, taking the precautions with which we had by now become familiar in this sort of situation. The sandstorm turned out to be a minor one, and we were soon on the move again. My look-out on the passenger side of our vehicle shouted out, "Sand from vehicle movement at 90 degrees." It was known that both enemy patrols and our own ranged far and wide behind each other's lines.

Looking through my field glasses I observed a lone 15cwt truck which appeared to be British. As we got closer we could see it was not an enemy patrol but one of our own Bedford wagons. The driver and his armourer mate jumped out of the cab with relief, "We've been lost for two days and are we glad to see you." "How did you get lost?" "Several Khamseens came down and all the track was lost, just nothing but sand." It was obvious they were terrified of the desert. It appeared they tagged on to two more vehicles making for the same unit. "When the Khamseen came on us it lasted a long time. We thought we could see the truck ahead of us for quite a way but when the sand storm cleared there was no one in sight and we were all on our own." I said to him, "You know the instructions when overtaken by a Khamseen – you stop and wait until it has cleared." "Yes, I know, but I thought we could see the truck ahead and when it had cleared we were all on our own." They had obviously been panic stricken. I said, "Why didn't you drive north and you would have been in line for Tobruk, and possibly met other trucks? To keep going south could have landed you in the Sand Sea." (The Sand Sea is an area of very soft sand, difficult to negotiate). At this he said, "How do I know which is south?" I was amazed. "Don't you know the sun rises in the east and sets in the west? If you go north you will eventually meet the main tracks which follow the coastline." I then added sarcastically, "If you miss the main tracks you will fall into the sea, then you will know where you are." This was a case of an urban dweller with no sense of direction having been overawed by the vastness and loneliness of the desert and unable to think logically under pressure.

During the last days of our 'residence' in Tobruk we were completely surrounded by the enemy and suffered shelling by day and bombing by night. The night bombing in particular meant that the shock waves from the bombs weakened the sides of our dugouts, causing the sand to cave in and swamp us. After one concentrated attack, I went out in the morning to a nearby abandoned Italian supply dump which contained a number of light Balsa wood coffins. As fervent Catholics, the Italians were more concerned about the niceties of death than the British. Our burial method was to dig a hole and drop the body into it with a piece of wood to act as a marker (if we could find one), then to fix one of the deceased's identity discs on it. The Graves Registration and Burial Unit would later be advised to reclaim the body and re-bury it in the main Military Cemetery in Tobruk.

Having loaded the truck with these Italian coffins and returned to camp, we cut apertures in the lids to act as breathing holes. We bedded down in these coffins and were able to sleep in relative comfort. It also proved that none of us were superstitious; death was now accepted far more lightly than it had been in civilian life.

In 1942, the toughest part of desert life was the monotonous rations we were given. There was no refrigeration in the forward areas, which were often hundreds of miles from base. We did not even enjoy the luxury of bread and our staple diet was hard tack biscuits and bully beef. Occasionally we had biscuits spread with margarine and tinned jam or marmalade. A rare treat was biscuits crushed into a paste with condensed milk and cooked. The staple cooked meal was corned beef (bully beef), tinned potatoes and crushed biscuits. When the N.A.A.F.I. wagon arrived once a month, if we were lucky, we would have a luxury feast of bully, followed by Australian pineapple chunks spooned straight out of the can, and a mug of hot tea with two teaspoons of sugar and condensed milk, so strong that the spoon almost stood up in the mug.

In spite of the conditions we were living under, I never had any problems sleeping. I would make myself as comfortable as possible in the dugout, close my eyes and I was away – only to be awakened by the Luftwaffe making themselves a nuisance nightly by flying overhead dropping showers of anti-personnel bombs, together with a few heavies in case the others had not woken us up. The important survival technique was to get below ground level and then only a direct hit would concern us. I usually slept through all the clatter.

During the day our training became more intensified as information trickled through to us that a 'big push', to be made by both sides, was imminent. Although we were some distance from the front line we could hear plainly the rattle of machine gun fire and the crump of mortars. The noises were clearer at night when on watch. I was thankful for having been supplied with a pair of Patrol Mark 1 desert boots (Army designation). These were suede boots with a thick man-made sole, which meant that we could move noiselessly at night. When the troops went on leave to Cairo they could be seen drinking heavily and meandering in their desert boots through the brothel area. The boots quickly became known as 'brothel creepers'.

One night when sound asleep I was suddenly awakened by the rattle of machine guns and the crack of hand grenades. Grabbing my rifle and 'pushing one up the spout', I peered over the top of the slit trench. Multi-coloured star shells sailed overhead, and dim forms moved around. A German patrol had penetrated our lines. At first light we discovered spent ammunition and a Verey pistol.

After this episode, life was to become different. Colonel Gore took over command of our unit. He was a giant of a man, six feet three inches tall, sporting a thick black moustache, and with a voice that roared like a bull. Gore was as mad as a hatter. His first orders were that we should do half an hour's infantry drill at sun up. From our point of view, this was absolutely crazy, as we were often subject to early morning attacks by Messerschmitts of the Luftwaffe. Gore insisted his orders be carried out. The following morning, just after dawn, I had lined the unit up and gone through the procedure of left right, left right, about turn, when Colonel Gore's staff car came speeding towards us in a cloud of dust. He stood, legs akimbo, watching our performance. I heard the whine of the early morning Luftwaffe patrol approaching fast. The men began to fall out of line and make for any handy holes. I looked up and saw a flight of three Messerschmitts heading straight for us. They had observed from afar the cloud of sand dust rising from Gore's car. "Stand fast," roared the Colonel, then, "Wait for my bloody orders." Within seconds the fighters were firing among us, with bullets zipping around everywhere. From my slit trench I looked up and saw Gore shouting at the top of his voice, "Get back on parade the lot of you." As I have written above, he was mad. Later when Tobruk fell, he rushed forward, his .45 revolver in hand, up to a leading German tank. The tank Commander calmly opened fire with his machine gun and shot off Gore's hand. This did not come as a surprise to us. After the war we learned that he had been repatriated from a P.O.W. Camp, but also that he was in the D-day landings and the vessel he was in hit a mine and 'Lucky Gore' was the only survivor.

On the 26th May 1942 Rommel was the first to attack. A 'ding dong' battle ensued for about 10 days. Squadrons of planes from both sides came over and the only ones falling out of the sky appeared to be British. The rumble of artillery fire and the continual flash of heavy guns came nearer to us. I had to take a 15cwt truck with some spares for the tanks of the 8th Hussars. Breasting an escarpment I found myself with a grandstand view of the terrible battle being fought. I never reached the unit I was trying to help, because they were involved in defending one of General Ritchie's famous 'boxes'. These consisted of tanks, artillery and infantry drawn up in box form on the flat desert waiting for the German 15th and 21st Panzer Divisions to drive into the areas between our 'boxes', where we would be able annihilate them with the combined fire from several 'boxes' at once. From my vantage point it was a fearsome sight to see the charging tanks and rippling gun flashes through the haze of bursting shells, smoke and dust. It was a sobering thought to realise that there below me thousands of men were locked in a life and death struggle.

Fig: 16. British 6 pound anti-tank gun in action on the open desert before Tobruk.

Lines of 'B' vehicles (R.A.S.C. supply wagons) were pulling out of the maelstrom and heading in our direction. This action, done to save as much as possible of the supplies brought up for the battle, made it evident to me that we were losing. Our forces were in headlong retreat. This was brought home forcibly to me, when a number of German 88mm guns, the scourge of the 8th Army, opened up towards us. These guns were able to completely out-range our own guns. The shells from the '88s came tearing past us at a frightening speed, following a completely flat trajectory, which appeared to carry on into eternity. I could only imagine what it was like for all those unfortunate comrades of ours who were on the receiving end of this barrage, below us on the battlefield.

Fig: 17. Rommel up with his troops during the assault on Tobruk. The pressure under which he commanded throughout the desert war clearly shows, even when triumph was within his grasp.

Arriving back at our lines in Tobruk, I reported to Captain Smith, informing him that in my opinion we were losing the battle, and it looked as if Tobruk would once again come under siege. "Well," he said, "I have just heard the B.B.C. news and they say we are winning the battle." Smith was really a dead loss, totally incapable of handling this type of situation. I realised there and then, that if I was to serve under this officer in siege conditions, it was going to be a bleak outlook for us all. It was quite apparent that he was already losing his nerve. I also knew that when the 'chips are down', with death and destruction all around, the ones who are highly strung like Smith were not the ones to have around you. I had already experienced that at Dunkirk.

Later that day the whole British 8th Army appeared to be streaming through and along the coastal track skirting our positions. The traffic was so busy that vehicles were being driven in line abreast to get to the rear as quickly as possible. I talked to members of the 4th Indian Division as they pulled up to draw water from us. They had suffered huge casualties in the Cauldron, as that battle had so aptly been named. They vividly described to us the conditions of hell as the infantry had been caught in the open and had to face hordes of German armour and heavy guns. I now realised there would be no stopping the Afrika Corps until they reached the Egyptian border. Captain Smith started to develop a nervous twitch. I felt sorry for him.

We bedded down that night to the rumbling of tank engines, half-tracks, gun limbers and lorries crowded with infantry that had survived the battle. After only a short sleep I was awakened by Captain Smith. He told me he had been down to Garrison H.Q. to see Colonel Gore who told him that only 80 men of the unit were to remain at Tobruk. "Tell Winter I want him to pick those who can stand the heat in the kitchen," he said. As the Sergeant Major had gone 'bomb happy' (our term for a man suffering shell shock), he was being evacuated and I was detailed to take over. I wished the Colonel had ordered Captain Smith to go too. I now had to face the forthcoming battle with him and his twitch, which would certainly intensify when the shelling started in earnest.

At daybreak the traffic became lighter and was able to move faster, throwing up suffocating clouds of sand. The drivers, realising that Messerschmitts were circling overhead looking for targets, were continuously zigzagging in their tracks. On one occasion when there was a gap in the traffic, a lone 3-ton truck came charging along the track. For some reason known only to the driver, he carried on in a straight line instead of taking a zigzag route. We saw a Messerschmitt go into a shallow dive, releasing a small silver coloured bomb, which landed smack on the top of the vehicle, leaving it a smouldering wreck. Joe, a laconic Lancastrian took his pipe out of his mouth and merely said, "It serves the bugger right, he should have known better than to drive in a straight line." Joe was one of the men who could stand the heat in the kitchen, the ones I wanted around me. Signals were arriving advising us to stock up rations and ammo close to hand, and our own initiative told us to dig even deeper.

The opinion amongst us all as we continued digging was 'Well, it's all for real now'.

As the gunfire crept closer, the traffic ceased except for a few ambulances. We were spared aerial attacks, the German pilots now concentrating on the exit routes from the perimeter. Along with the heavy rumble of bombs, we saw long rising plumes of smoke in the direction of El Adem. Joe remarked, "I'm glad it's them and not us. Keep it over there, Jerry." Late that afternoon everything quietened down in our sector. All the battle noise was now far off and all we could hear was the clanging of picks and shovels as troops, stripped to the waist, toiled away in the desert heat. I made a 'recce' with a few men up to the escarpment at our rear and found a cave, which had obviously been used by the Italians in the past. An entrance had been covered with netting. Deciding this would be our bolthole if the worst came to the worst, we stocked it with tinned food and then doused it in flea powder as protection against the Libyan sand fleas, which were very virulent.

At mid-morning the next day, I was sitting in my deepened foxhole feeling pleasurably comfortable, when a large group of German aircraft came over and heavily bombed the harbour area. As they headed back towards their base, one aircraft dropped a stick of bombs on our position, which was close to a junction of several tracks. There being no roads in the area, tracks were very important. One specific order given to us was, "Look for unexploded bombs and mark them with wooden sticks surmounted by a skull and crossbones sign." Very few time bombs were being used at that stage in the campaign. So if bombs did not explode on contact, they were obviously 'duds'. In the soft sand their positions were easily recognisable by the depression they had made as they plunged into the sand. It was therefore important to mark them as instructed. If heavy traffic such as a tank transporter carrying a tank to the rear to be repaired passed over the spot, it could easily trigger the bomb.

Captain Smith and myself had worked out a rota for this duty – 12hour stints. On this particular day I was not on duty. After an interval, there being no sign of the Captain, I walked over to his slit trench and found him disinterested. "What about marking the bombs?" I said to him. "You do it," was his reply. "Not on your Nelly, it's your turn of duty," I told him. "I've changed the rota, you do it now and that's an order," Smith said. "Is it just the fact that you are scared and will be the same tomorrow?" "I'll have you on a charge if you speak to me like that." All the troops around could hear this exchange. Heads were popping up out of trenches with remarks flying around such as, "You tell him to f... off." This was not good for discipline, so I said, "Who's coming with me?" A couple of the men came and we marked the depressions. As I went back, I looked down into his slit trench, Smith was sitting just staring blankly into space. And the battle had not yet begun!

That evening there was a non-stop German artillery barrage, continuing throughout the night. Fortunately, none of the shells reached into our position as the 15th and 21st Panzer Divisions were pounding away, their aim being to penetrate our perimeter and achieve a breakthrough to our rear.

A dispatch rider came up the escarpment to tell us it was believed there would be a German attack at dawn. We were already aware of that. As dawn broke, the rumbling of enemy artillery fire came nearer. After a few hours we could hear the now familiar clanking noise of approaching tanks. I crawled my way to the top of the escarpment and could see that the German tanks had over-run the 25pounder guns of the 2nd South African Division.

Evidently the first line of defence, the infantry, had been overrun and the second defensive line of artillery had also been captured. We had been expected to 'mop up' any odd surviving German units attempting to penetrate our line. Our Boyes anti-tank rifles were designed to be effective against targets much 'softer' than the Panzers we now faced. We were now alone and facing the approaching hordes of tanks, which now fanned out with an ear-splitting noise and churned up clouds of sand. We crouched down in our trenches as far as possible, hoping for the best. The tanks continued to sweep past and, hoping that the infantry had not closed up, we jumped out and made our way through the swirling sand and up to our cave.

I dived in through the entrance of the cave and became entangled in the covering netting. Picking myself up and looking around, I was thankful to see that everyone under my command was there, we had suffered no casualties – only a loss of pride. After a while, I cautiously lifted up the netting to see the Panzer Grenadiers advancing in a line abreast, lobbing the occasional hand grenade into caves. I turned back to the others saying, "When they get here, it's curtains for us." Everyone agreed. One final thing I did before leaving was to open a tin of South African coffee and stir some flea powder in it. This was our farewell gesture to the Germans.

Fig: 18. The Mk IV Panzer tank. By the time of the fall of Tobruk, this was the standard German battle tank throughout the desert campaigns.

Trooping out of the cave we saw a lone Mark 4 Panzer tank, its Commander standing erect in the turret with his head and shoulders visible. As I walked towards him, he said in perfect English, "Ah, Engländers, for you the war is over. Have a Players cigarette." A phrase I shall never forget. While troop movements went backwards and forwards in the desert campaigns, each side revelled in raiding the other side's food dumps. The Germans' favourites were our Players cigarettes. Our favourites were their succulent Bavarian cheeses wrapped in silver paper. These delicacies were specially flown over from Greece and dropped to their forward troops who were given superior rations to those serving in the rear areas. The food rations supplied to us were the same for troops at the front line and those in rear areas.

Fig: 19. The port area of Tobruk immediately following the fall.

Fig: 20. The city of Tobruk immediately following the fall.

Fig: 21. British prisoners on the outskirts of Tobruk, waiting to be removed 'to the rear'.

'In The Bag'

All we P.O.W.s were marshalled together in a collecting area. We glanced at the bodies lying around among the smouldering vehicles that had been destroyed in the battle. As we approached a junction of several tracks we were brought to a halt. A German officer said to me, "Stay here, but get rid of those bloody black men." He was referring to a group of South African coloured troops. "Sorry," I said, "They are not under our command." He shrugged his shoulders and went to find a South African officer or N.C.O. Shortly afterwards, a small convoy of vehicles arrived. In the front vehicle, standing up and gripping the windscreen, was the German General, Erwin Rommel. Distinctive in his peaked hat instead of the normal Afrika Corps' cap, surmounted by a pair of sand goggles, he jumped down and began talking to a group of the British P.O.W.s, who smartly saluted him. He then climbed back into his staff car and with a friendly wave moved away. We respected the German General. Unlike his counterparts the British Generals, Rommel was always right up with his troops. Always close to the action.

We were directed to the collecting point. A couple of German 88mm guns set up nearby were pointing towards an area where a Battalion of British Cameron Highlanders, were still holding out. A German officer walked across to us and said, "Move back if you want to preserve your hearing." When the guns opened up it was ear shattering; the tremendous muzzle velocity almost lifted us off the ground. We pitied the poor Camerons as the guns' shells landed amongst them. Realising they had no hope, they came up out of their positions. Headed by the Battalion's Piper, they marched impressively in military formation towards captivity. Bloody, but unbowed and proud.

As the sounds of the fighting died away, we wearily laid ourselves down, terribly dispirited. Our world had collapsed. We were now to be subjected to taking orders from people we hated. We now had to think about the future – if we had one. There was a feeling of shame at being captured. Then came the realisation that from now onwards life was going to be very empty. This was the second defeat I had experienced. At Dunkirk I had the desolate fear of being taken as a prisoner of war. It had not happened then, and I had survived when it had appeared all was lost.

Now the 8th Army was hundreds of miles away near Cairo. Worst of all the German Afrika Corps had become a strong, well-equipped and confident force. How could we possibly survive against such strength? If Rommel were to take the Suez Canal, then all would be lost. In addition, the Germans were now fighting and winning on the Russian front. There must be a ray of hope somewhere we thought. Well, hope springs eternal in the human breast.

Early Days As A P.O.W.

So I took stock of myself. What did I possess?
One standard issue short-sleeved bush shirt
One standard issue pair of shorts
One standard issue pair of underpants
One pair of desert boots
One pair of woollen socks
One handkerchief
Two softback books I had grabbed up on impulse as I leapt out of the gun pit: Palgrave's Golden Treasury and Pitman's Shorthand Textbook

I had no blankets, no pillow, no toothbrush, and no comb. In fact, literally nothing but what I stood up in. I would have to sleep with my head in my cupped hands and brush my teeth with my index finger. I did have a steel helmet, but later, when I was being handed over to the Italians, it was snatched from me as a souvenir. What I did have, though, was an implacable will to survive.

As darkness fell over Tobruk it appeared unreal. Fires flickered from burning equipment. Ammunition was exploding among the fires, and the pungent smell of burning tanks and their human occupants permeated the air.

For months I had slept on the ground wrapped in a blanket. It was no longer a hardship. The desert campaign had toughened me and now I didn't even have a blanket. The desert was very hot during daylight hours but extremely cold at night. On the very first night of captivity I managed to read a few pages of Palgrave's Golden Treasury before the daylight failed and sleep took over, despite the drop in temperature.

On the second day, as more P.O.W.s crowded into our area, we realised there had been more men in the Garrison than we had thought. I had recently risen to the rank of Sergeant Major, if only temporarily. My promotion had been given to me a few days before the battle, but no record had survived, so I was officially back to being a Staff Sergeant once more. So far I had been caught up in the fighting at Dunkirk, sailed around the Cape to Egypt, served in Palestine, and finally lived a hard existence in the desert. Within the next few years I was to look back and realise that in June 1942, I was relatively 'a babe in arms'. Before the end of the war I was to see many men die, both physically and mentally. I listened to others baring their souls as they had never done before, whilst slowly but surely losing their reason. Some men I learned to trust, some to distrust, some to despise, and some to admire and respect. One dominant feature from now on was the realisation that we had to hang on to our sense of humour, which would transcend the many grim and dangerous situations we found ourselves in.

We realised that one of the problems we were going to have to contend with was spending days without shelter in the searing sun. Before our capture, when moving about in convoy, we could lie in the shade under our vehicles when we stopped for a break. Now we were going to be exposed to the sun from the moment it came up until the very second it disappeared over the western horizon. We found that after many months of sun exposure to our bodies, our skin had turned brown. It was now going to turn an even deeper shade of brown, making us virtually indistinguishable from the Indian troops amongst us. We also yearned for a bowl of water and a bar of soap. Some of the P.O.W.s did have soap but there was no water for washing – it was strictly rationed and reserved for drinking.

Such a large number of prisoners had been taken when the Garrison collapsed, that although there were sufficient stocks of food held in reserve at Tobruk, we had not yet been given permission to retrieve them. The Germans were relying on these stocks to alleviate their own supply shortages. I was somewhat surprised to discover a number amongst us who appeared to be quite phlegmatic at the situation we were in. This was perhaps borne out of the fact that they had been in the desert a long time, when the campaigns had flowed forwards and backwards across the desert. At one stage, we came to be known as the 'Benghazi Harriers'.

There were a number of the men with us who, having only just been posted to the forward areas, had no time to acclimatise themselves to the horrors and discomforts of war and suffered badly. Unable to accept the conditions we were now experiencing, many of these men just gave up. Having acquired the ability to look straight into a man's eyes, I was able to know if he was telling me the truth – whether he was in genuine pain, or whether the grey matter behind his eyes was dying out. Later, on more than one occasion when in Italy, the Medical Officer would look at a lifeless body and say to me, "I can find nothing positive which has caused this man's death." Psychologically, the most testing time for a P.O.W. is the first month of captivity. We would say, "Stick that out and you can then stand it for years."

A temporary P.O.W. Camp in a forward area is referred to as a 'cage'. We had been incarcerated in the 'cage' at Tobruk for a couple of weeks, when a German Oberleutnant came to us and said in faultless English, "Very sorry you chaps, but I'm afraid we must hand you over to the Italians, because we have to push on as soon as possible and chase your comrades into Egypt." He was supremely confident of victory. One of our chaps looked the German straight in the eye and said, "Don't forget that the British have a reputation of always winning the last battle." This abruptly concluded the conversation.

The German Officer returned to speak to me personally, "I notice that you are wearing an Australian bush hat. If I were you I would bury it before the Italians arrive." I suddenly remembered why he had made that remark and thanked him. I knew that in a previous battle fought between the Australian Infantry and the Italians, the 'Aussies' had overrun the Italian positions with a bayonet charge. Before their adrenaline had worn off, they also bayoneted some Italians who were holding their hands up. In a counter attack the Italians learned of this and vowed revenge on any Australians they might capture. I quickly disposed of my treasured bush hat under a pile of stones. The Italians duly arrived and their first question was, "Are there any Australians here?" These Italians were a slovenly lot, evidently base troops brought in to tidy up after the fighting.

Our small group was joined by a chap called Charlie. We felt sorry for the lad who, we realised, was suffering from shell shock brought on by the recent fighting in which he had been involved. He was constantly looking behind him and had also developed a nervous twitch. We spent a lot of our time trying to help Charlie.

The Italians arrived with a convoy of trucks and trailers. We were bundled on board them amidst shouts of, "Avanti, avanti, presto, presto." They were not just concerned with loading us on board, but continued to press us tighter and tighter. We finished up packed like a tin of sardines. The searing sun beating down added to our discomfort. Iron stanchions connected with heavy chains were fixed round the trailers. Some of the troops were unfortunate enough to be packed on the outer fringes of the trailer wedged against the chains, with only the material of their bush shirts to protect them.

On the move, the Italian driver was trying to show his driving expertise by not bothering to avoid the numerous potholes. We swayed in a solid mass from side to side. The ones wedged against the chains were suffering in agony and we had a long journey and several hundred miles ahead. Clouds of sand whirled around and up into our faces as the merciless sun beat down.

Eventually we stopped at a waterhole, which was a welcome relief. During the journey four men in the trailer died. We were given entrenching tools by the Italian guards, which we used to bury the bodies by the side of the track.

By now Charlie was in a bad state. He had arrived in our lines after being involved in the initial German attack on the outer perimeter of Tobruk. Many of his comrades had been killed and Charlie was so shattered he did not know where he was. We put him in the middle of the trailer saying to him, "Cheer up Charlie, there's more room for us now." He was in no condition to appreciate that comment. As the afternoon wore on, we realised that Charlie would not survive the journey. He died quietly, looking at us with a weak smile. He closed his eyes and he was gone. He was so tightly wedged against us that he didn't drop down but remained standing up. We stopped a few miles from Derna and buried Charlie together with four more who had died.

One of my Corporals came to me and said, "Charlie said at the last stop that if anything happened to him he would like you to drop a line to his old mum with all the standard comment about a hero's death." "O.K., if Charlie wanted me to do that, I will." The Corporal handed me a letter from Charlie's mother in Colchester. As I lay on the ground that night I stared at the jewelled pattern of stars slowly climbing across the velvet sky and began to think what I would write. I had done it before, but for Charlie, and to his mother, I would write something special. I put his mother's letter together with Charlie's identity disc in my helmet, and placed it by my side before drifting off to sleep.

The next morning we were awake early and preparing to board the trucks when there was an almighty commotion. Sporadic firing had broken out. It was rumoured that a lone Long Range Desert Group scout car had attempted to turn the convoy back. An Italian armoured car had appeared and driven it away. In the confusion we were bundled speedily aboard the trucks. I then realised I had forgotten to bring the letter with Charlie's mother's address. I couldn't remember the address and neither could the Corporal. I vowed that after the war I would make some enquiries and do something about it. I was saddened to know that all Charlie's mother would receive was a black-edged notification, 'Missing – Lost in action'. She deserved better.

At the next stop we had to bury some more of the dead – I forget how many. One of the guards pointed to the place where we should dig. We disagreed and pointed to an area of softer sand. A violent argument took place with gesticulations flying around until an Italian Sergenti Majori arrived and agreed to our suggestion. We placed one of each man's identity discs on to a lone piece of wood, saving the others to pass on to the Italian Red Cross.

The area we were now passing through was more pleasant than Tobruk and quite green after the brown of the desert. We were off-loaded near a crystal clear spring running into what appeared, by the carvings on the stone, to be an old Roman cistern. To us, this was the absolute lap of luxury. We could now have our first wash for over a week. We realised that any small improvements would make all the difference to the quality of whatever life we were to have. With a few palm trees scattered around we organised a rota to lie in the shade of them, not realising we were organising ourselves to the benefit of all. These early lessons learned when the 'chips were down' have been imprinted on me all my life.

I started to suffer from 'desert sores', a common problem from being in the desert. When the sores were suppurating I kept walking around to brush off the multitude of irritating flies. Finally, I had to lie on my back most of the time, which was far from comfortable.

We were given the rations of one large biscuit per day (we called them dog biscuits), a stern test for our teeth. Also, we received one small tin of what we believed was mule meat, to be shared between five of us. This meagre concession made our spirits rise. At least we were alive.

Suddenly there was a flurry of activity on the Camp amongst the Italians. We could observe them blancoing their equipment and brushing their uniforms, cleaning up, and even sweeping around their quarters. We had in our military careers experienced the same activity when a V.I.P. was due to visit our own camps. We tried with our very limited knowledge of the Italian language to find out what was going on, but the guards had obviously been sworn to secrecy. When the word Mussolini was mentioned, the guard put his finger to his mouth. So that was it. We immediately formed a Camp Committee. If we were to be honoured by a visit from the Duce, then surely we ought to give him a rousing reception in a good old English way. We laid our plans accordingly, especially when we saw two large cine cameras being erected near the Main Gates, and a team of cameramen lounging around each one.

In the meantime, we moved around the Camp picking up stones to fill our pockets. In the distance we could see a group of uniformed officers wearing their best blues, not the normal khaki drill, strolling up and down. An extra supply of meat had been handed to us to celebrate the occasion. A detachment of troops appeared and was actually marching in step to take up their positions. A further number of rotund officers, their uniforms glinting in blue and gold, appeared.

We gathered at the Main Gate, this was the moment we had waited for. As arranged, we prepared to take aim as the V.I.P. party moved towards us. We knew that it would be too dangerous if we left our 'welcome' until they were too close, as the guards might open fire on us. Sergeant Major Cameron in charge shouted, "Let 'em have it." And we did. A fusillade of sharp stones sailed through the air, thudding into the ground making puffs of sand in front of the approaching party, who stopped dead in confusion. The officer in charge of the escorting party shouted an order to his troops to fire, which they did half-heartedly in the air. The camera crews had already fled to safety as we let go another volley of stones. From where I was standing, I did not have a clear view of Mussolini but the ones at the front did. Satisfied with the 'welcome' we had given their beloved Duce, we retired in good order and sat down on the ground. Later, we were told by the guards that Mussolini had come over to North Africa to inspect his victorious troops, travelling as far forward as Tobruk.

After the stone-throwing episode, it quietened down until a heavily armed party came through the Main Gate, escorting a number of workmen to the lovely cistern from where we had got our drinking water, and tipping buckets of excreta into it. When the Italian interpreter shouted that it served us right, he appeared quite puzzled as we stood around laughing as loud as we could. This kept our spirits up, also knowing what a tale we would have to tell – having thrown stones at Mussolini! One lesson we had learned was that, faced with provocation, the Italians would never open fire into a Camp of defenceless prisoners. Whatever we thought about the Italians as enemies, they would never be as ruthless as the Germans in the same circumstances. For several days we were without water, unable to risk drinking from the polluted spring. We put chlorine tablets in and after a few days we decided it was O.K.

The next move, having left the desert tracks behind us, took us along the coast road to Benghazi. Arriving in an area just outside the city, we remained there for two weeks and became an object of curiosity for both the local Arabs and Italians, who seemed annoyed when we raised our fingers to them in derision. But to our delight it was very effective. The Camp was a hell-hole and the Italians did nothing about the conditions. Dysentery raged through the Camp like wildfire. It was tragic to see so many fine soldiers writhing in agony. We had to dig our own latrine pits at the far end of the Camp, putting wooden poles across them to straddle the pits. These cesspits would be occupied all day, with some poor wretches becoming weaker until they fell in. Not having supplies of water to wash them down, we went and stood by the Main Gate and shouted at the top of our voices. Eventually we were supplied with water. At least the overwhelming stench kept the civilians away from the wire. We then had the problem of coping with millions of flies, which produced a serious health hazard for us. While drinking the daily ration of macaroni soup out of an aluminium 'dixie', we had to cup our hands over it or we would have swallowed flies by the hundreds. A number of the men became so weak that they began to pass blood regularly. They were taken away by Italian medical staff on an ancient cart without springs, pulled by a thin, sad-looking donkey. We wondered how many of those men survived that terrible journey along the pot-holed road.

We cheered when the Italians scattered in panic as a squadron of R.A.F. Boston bombers appeared and proceeded to bomb the nearby harbour. The Italians then came out of their shelter to gleefully remind us that we would soon be shipped from Benghazi to Italy. That news caused us great concern for we knew that when a ship load of us passed through the docks, with the Italians' normal 'efficiency', we could well become the target of our own bombers.

We then had one of the few strokes of luck. One of the P.O.W.s amongst us had served in a Long Range Desert Group. (These men, when operating behind enemy lines, had been attired in Arab clothes). He came to us saying that he had recognised one of the Arabs passing along the wire as a member of one of the recce patrols he had been on. He told us that the Arab would be passing on intelligence information to the G.H.Q that we were awaiting shipment through Benghazi.

The British air raids continued frequently until the day we moved. Ordered out of the Camp early one morning we shuffled in our desert boots, raising clouds of sand dust as we moved along the track towards the dock. We hoped that this would alert the L.R.D.G., which it did because no bombers appeared as we were taken through the docks.

We halted beside an empty freighter, the "Nino Bixio" of Genoa. As we boarded the ship we looked with anxious eyes skyward, but thankfully no bombers appeared. Herded into the bowels of the ship by climbing down slippery steel ladders, we had to lie on stinking and dirty hot plates. One soldier sat next to me said 'his prayers had been answered'. He was entitled to that opinion.

The following morning found us sailing across the Mediterranean. The ship was zigzagging and travelling at maximum speed, with the engines going flat out, which had the whole ship shuddering violently. The conditions below, with oven temperature heat, were foul, although the hatch cover over our heads was open and we could see fighter aircraft in the sky above us, which meant there was little likelihood of us being bombed.

Dysentery was still prevalent among us. Conditions continued to get worse until the crew allowed us to go up the ladders and on to the deck to relieve the calls of nature. We had to try and pick the right time to go up the ladder. If we followed a chap who was suffering badly from dysentery, we would be very likely to become covered with his excrement before we reached the top of the ladder. On arriving on the deck it was wonderful to feel the sea air, and it was a relief when we were hosed down to get rid of the filth in which we were all covered.

Looking out over the rails I could see we were being protected by an escort of four destroyers, and also by patrolling aircraft. This made us only slightly less uneasy, knowing there could be Royal Navy submarines active in these waters. That would be the reason why the Italians employed such a large escort for such a small convoy. Later that day we heard a loud explosion, which caused the 'Nino Bixio' to take evasive action, throwing us on top of one another. We realised that one of the vessels from our convoy had been hit by a British naval torpedo. We hoped it had been one of the escorts and not the other P.O.W. vessel. Sadly, on arrival at Brindisi, we saw that ours was the only P.O.W. vessel docked there. We realised that once again we had been lucky. Later on, at a P.O.W. Camp in Italy, I met a soldier who had been on the other ship. He said he had been lying on the ship's plates when there was a loud explosion, and the next thing he knew was that he found himself swimming in the sea.

Italy

On arriving at Brindisi, we found it to be dirty and smelly. In many ways it had the air of an African rather than a European town. When we were formed up on the dockside, the Italian stevedores pelted us with whatever they could lay their hands on. We were totally helpless and unable to retaliate. Little did we know then that there was even worse to come. We were taken through a slum area of narrow streets, the houses four storeys high, with lines of washing strung out from the balconies. The women came out and bombarded us with household rubbish. From their balconies they couldn't miss us and tomatoes came hurtling down. We tried to catch them or scrape them off our heads. Onions were the easiest to catch and we regarded them as delicacies, not having tasted fresh vegetables for months – in fact, not since being stationed in the desert. One wit amongst us shouted out, "Everything but the kitchen sink has landed on my head." He may have been tempting fate with that remark.

Arriving in the Piazza beyond the slum quarter, everything changed. A stentorian bellow rang out, "Halt." A voice of authority, and all of us, including the Italian guards, halted. It was Sergeant Major Cameron of the Camerons. He was a wonderful character, short, stocky and every inch a professional soldier. He had served in India for many years and was possessed of an iron will and strong determination. He was a born leader of men. His voice rang out to a silent crowd, "Let us show these bloody 'Eyeties' that we are the conquering Desert Rats. Come on. Chests out, chins up, shoulders back, and when I give the word of command you will all step off with the left foot and we will sing that famous British Army song which has been heard through the ages, and throughout the world – *The British Grenadiers*". Every one of us came to attention, then we shuffled into threes. Next came the Sergeant Major's command of, "Attention. Byyyyy the left – quick march, left right, left right, all together now."

"Some talk of Alexander and some talk of Hercules,
of Hector and Lysander and such great names as these,
but of all the world's great heroes, there's none that can compare,
with a tow row, tow row, tow row row, of the British Grenadiers."

Every voice was in full-throated song, echoing with pride round the square. The Italians, guards and civilians alike, looked on in amazement. Cameron's spirit spread down the ranks like wildfire, and once again they were composed of fighting men. That heart-warming scene will remain in my memory forever. We marched off and as we reached the outskirts of the town, Cameron shouted, "Ease off lads," which we were relieved to do. We were worn out with marching and singing.

Later in the day we reached our first Italian Camp at Tintirano, near Brindisi on the heel of Italy, known as Campo Concentramento No. 65. It was sited on a bleak hill, surrounded by a bare stony area with hardly a tree in sight. One consolation was that it would catch any stray wind cooling the camp, for it was devilish hot and we could only lounge in the shade of the huts. Our internment in Italy had finally begun. The Camp consisted of 6 ramshackle breeze-block built Huts, each accommodating about 300 British, South African and Indian troops. The Huts were windowless and draughty, and during the following winter of 1942 they were to be the miserable and cheerless home of almost 2,000 P.O.W.s. The majority of the men had served in the 7th Armoured Division (Desert Rats), the 4th Indian Division, the 50th (Northumbrian) Division, and a mixed bag of other troops, all of whom had been captured in North Africa. Before our capture, we had regarded ourselves as the crack fighting troops of the British Army. Many among us were regular soldiers who had seen much active service; a number were Territorial Army soldiers, proud of being volunteers; and a few were conscripts.

Long periods in the Western Desert, living in gun pits, sleeping on the ground under the stars, and existing on bully beef and biscuits had made us into a tough breed able to look after ourselves.

However, morale was at a very low ebb, following our capture and the initial loss of men through dysentery and the starvation rations at Benghazi. There was also a steady flow of bad news from the fighting still going on, with reverses for the Allies in both North Africa and Russia. Some mornings we found the stiff corpses of men in their bunks where they had literally just given up and died. Looking at them we remarked, "They couldn't stand the heat in the kitchen."

Nothing, however, could hide our anti-Italian feeling. We had beaten them in the desert until the Germans appeared in order to stiffen and reinforce their army, and they would never possess a moral ascendancy over us. And they knew it. We were not receiving any Red Cross parcels, although we had been told there was a warehouse full of them in Brindisi. We were fed up of picking whole chestnuts and acorns out of our bread ration. The two bowls of soup per man, per day, were merely made of slops of macaroni spread, over-ripe sludgy tomatoes, vegetables and stale bread rolls.

At this stage (early September 1942) I began to wonder what the future held for me. The last three months had been horrific and I consoled myself with the thought that the future could not be any worse than the past.

One chap commented, "What will happen to us if we lose the war and have to spend years in P.O.W. camps followed by years of slave labour under the Nazis?" I replied to him angrily, "If I hear you make that comment again, I'll thump you – hard. We must all be positive about the future as we are now in a survival game, and the weaklings who talk like that will quickly go to the wall."

What a traumatic period we had all gone through. We had watched helplessly as many of our friends just stopped breathing. That may sound a terribly casual statement, but after what we had suffered we had become as hard as nails. We were different men from those who had embarked on the troopship in England destined for the Middle East. Now at 23 years of age, I had become a much more mature person. Most of us were of a similar age to myself, but there was one 'old codger' amongst us – a Sergeant Major in his late thirties. We called him 'Dad'.

Before I was captured or, as we say in army parlance, 'whipped into the bag', life in the desert had been hard. We had lived in holes in the ground, or in a cave at Tobruk, with no bed, just a pillow and two coarse blankets, and had coped with the uncomfortable khamseen and the millions of sand fleas. Meals consisted of meat and veg, balancing a dixie can while sitting cross-legged. Life in the cave had actually been relatively luxurious, as we had the use of an old packing case as a table.

Our first night in captivity at Tobruk was the worst, for although the temperature in the day was about 100 degrees, it dropped sharply at night. We slept close together with our bare knees up to our chins. Until our arrival in Italy we were constantly hungry. It was through those months of hard living that I became inured to hardship. At Benghazi we had only the ground to sleep on, without even a blanket or pillow. We were told by the Italians that we would be issued with them when we reached Italy.

As a P.O.W. I realised that everything in life is relative. My position had now slightly improved. I was sleeping in a three-tiered bunk bed, with bed boards and a straw-filled mattress and pillow. At first the pillow was uncomfortable because, when I moved my head, the crackling of the straw particles seemed to become magnified. As the straw became ground down it became compressed and the noise ceased, but then I had a flat pillow. After an argument with the Italian Quartermaster, we were given new straw, but the noise of crackling straw returned. We couldn't win.

After being in the camp for three weeks we were invaded by an army of virulent bed bugs and fleas. We could now expect them to be followed by lice. We protested fiercely to be 'deloused'. The reply was, "Domani," which in Italian was 'tomorrow'. The following day we were told "Dopo Domani," meaning 'the day after tomorrow'. Then would come the word "Oggi". We came to understand that "Oggi" means 'in a few days', and "Domani" means 'about a week' and "Dopo Domani" means 'never'. I was now learning the finer nuances of the Italian language.

Since captivity we had always been desperately hungry, and hunger has a debilitating effect on morale. Our flimsy desert attire, which we had worn every day and slept in every night, was reduced to rags, giving us a Robinson Crusoe appearance. We were constantly being taunted by the Italian guards, boasting that when they had won the war, we would become their slave labourers in the New European Order, and we would never see our families in England again.

We knew that Rommel was poised to attack Egypt. Being old desert hands, we wondered how he could maintain his lines of communications. The Germans had conquered every Russian army they had faced, and if Moscow and Leningrad were to fall, how could the Russians survive? An enormous German army would then be in a position to invade England. The gist of our daily conversation was never to give up hope and to grasp at any straw which might bring hope. We were at our lowest point in morale. How long would we have to endure the conditions we were living in before we reached our climax of despair? We did not know.

The Camp Committee met and decided that we must:
(a) Prevent the spread of gloom and despair at all times.
(b) Take strong measures to maintain discipline at all times.

I was placed in charge of Hut No 1. Each morning at 7.00 a.m., I took a fatigue party to the cookhouse, collecting a quantity of black liquid called 'coffee'. We called it 'sludge'. No milk and no sugar. The last time I had tasted milk was in the Delta nine months previously. What we had collected was doled out to each syndicate of five men – everything was in fives. That was the Italian way of counting. At least the early morning drink was warming. A slice of dry bread would complete our breakfast.

At 9.00 a.m. a whistle would blow and the whole compliment of 2,000 P.O.W.s would shamble out and line up in some semblance of order to be counted. When it was cold we would stand there draped in our blankets looking like a group of Arabs. I was responsible for 300 men and by the time the Italian Adjutant arrived (late of course), we were cold, shivering, mumbling like a swarm of bees and glaring at the Italian Sergeant who counted us in a highly pitched monotone voice – "uno, due, tre, quattro" etc etc. With a bit of luck he would reach the grand total of 300 first time. We would mutter "buono". Each hut would be checked, the whistle would blow again and we would trudge back to our huts and our three-tiered bunks. Some to talk, some to sleep, while some simply stayed outside to drift aimlessly around the wire.

The wire. It was always there. Our whole lives revolved round it. It was indelibly imprinted on our entire outlook on life. This ever-present symbol of our status was eventually to send some men round the bend.

At noon another whistle would blow and I would take my party to the cookhouse to draw our ration of hot soup. This was a misnomer. We christened the stuff 'skilly'. It was basically vegetable soup. Some days it was thicker than normal, if there were more cabbage stalks in it. Great care was taken by the cook to measure it out exactly. Any second helpings would be issued to the first bay in the hut. On the next occasion the second bay and so forth. 300 pairs of eyes would watch the entire proceedings closely. Food was our survival.

In the afternoon we would sit by the wall of the hut, where a small sliver of winter sunshine had been soaked up by the wall. We would then pass our time by practising the delicate art of lice picking. By now everyone was harbouring lice. De-licing was by running the tips of one's fingers along the seam and cracking each individual louse. We were daily asking the Italians to bring a delousing machine into the camp. One did arrive, but only when a supply of British uniforms were delivered by the Red Cross.

At 5.00 p.m. the fatigue party was once again on its way to the cookhouse for another helping of 'skilly' and a mug of herb tea. This was supplemented by two slices of dry bread and a thimble full of jam. Until darkness fell, those with agile limbs strolled round the perimeter. Those with agile minds talked, the rest just lay in their bunks gazing at nothing. Another day had passed.

In November the cold, damp weather arrived. At night, sleeping in my tattered shirt with a thin Italian blanket wrapped round me, I would huddle in my bunk, knees up to my chest, the best way to keep warm.

As a treat on Sundays we were given a ration of cheese. The first time I collected it and was handed a roll of cheese by the Italian Quartermaster, he said to me, "Your ration for 300." I looked at him in amazement, "How can I cut 300 pieces from this?" "Easy," he said, "Just use this," handing me a length of piano wire and two pieces of wood. After some practice, I solved the problem by cutting the round lump of cheese in two, then halving it, then halving again and repeating the process until we had the right number of pieces. It was tasty and surprisingly filling.

As the summer months of 1942 drifted by and winter approached, the increasingly cold weather began to have a dispiriting effect on us. The morning Roll Call became tedious. Worst of all, the soles and uppers of my desert boots had finally parted company. I had to tie strips of rags around them to try and bring them together. When we were on parade, it often rained and, standing in puddles of mud, I could feel my sodden feet getting colder and colder. We became more cheerful when a rumour began to circulate round the camp that a lorry load of Red Cross parcels would be arriving soon. Eventually a lorry did arrive and we cheered as a large number of parcels were unloaded, then we were told by the Italians that the first ration would be one parcel to be shared between each group of five men.

Opening the parcel, we found it contained a tin of porridge, a tin of meat roll, tea, sugar and Klim (powdered milk), a block of chocolate and some cheese. We felt we were virtually in Paradise. The first thing was to make a brew of tea. While drinking it we began to plan the menu for the following week. Someone remarked, "What will it be like if we are issued with one parcel per man per week?" We fantasised. A notice posted up by the Quartermaster read, 'Should more Red Cross parcels arrive in due course, there may be an increase in the ration to one parcel per man per week'.

About this time I joined another group. David Syme from Melbourne in Australia, whose family owned a small shipping line, Gordon Bode, another 'Aussie' from Queensland, a farmer, Albert Robinson, a saxophone player from Durham, Bill Smith, a civil servant from Surrey, and I made up the five. Coming from such widely differing backgrounds, we spent the evenings in conversation recalling our military and civilian experiences.

For several months most of the food given to us had been liquids, which gave us all one problem – WIND. We had been existing on macaroni soup, creating excessive flatulence in everyone's body. One of our group, having spent many years serving in India, said that to break the monotony out there they would ignite the discharges of human methane gas, to see who could produce the longest flame. We could not believe this but decided to put it to the test. Not having any matches, I asked the interpreter if he could supply us with a box of matches. He was dumbfounded when we told him the reason, but he brought us the matches. A demonstration was given, which impressed everyone. Thin tight khaki trousers, ideal for the best results, were in good supply. Blue flames during sessions of practising could be observed in most huts. We were told that the Italians, having been told by the interpreter what we were up to, had begun to follow our example. The comment from Sergeant Major Cameron was, "Once again, as in past history, the British haveespread their culture throughout the world."

During practice sessions, a large group of men were huddled together, breaking wind continuously. In the evening we lay on our bunks listening to a loud variety of wind noises emitting in all keys from major to minor. One evening a voice chimed up, "Come on lads, at the count of three. One, two, three, break." The result was amazing. We found that we could now break wind at will and the final performance sounded like the last long drawn out chord from an out of tune decrepit Persian orchestra.

The harder we practised, the more controlled we became, so we decided to give an outside performance aimed against our enemies. As the Italian Corporal nominated to count us in the morning Roll Call passed down the line droning away, "uno, due, tre, quattro, etc," we all awaited impassively for the word of command as the Corporal reached number 10. Then Sergeant Major roared, "Fart," and the reply was instantaneous and loud.

The Corporal stopped, hand to nose, in astonishment, hesitated momentarily, then started to count again. Reaching number 10 there was a boisterous fusillade of different pitched wind noises. We had expertly timed our wind releasing skill, achieving perfection. As was to be expected, the Adjutant came dashing out of his office to see what was going on. We had reserved our greatest effort to greet him in a suitable manner, but his sense of humour was not moved by our efforts. On this occasion we did not break into laughter, but let our movements speak for ourselves. Sad to say, when further Red Cross parcels arrived and we were consuming solid foods once more, we found that our early achievements could never again be matched.

Daily Life In Italy

In the early days of P.O.W. life, one always had a terrible feeling of frustration at being so utterly cut off from the mainstream of war. At the back of our minds was a gnawing feeling, which we never expressed. Perhaps the Italian and German propaganda was right that they would launch some of their secret weapons about which they were always hinting? So far, with our inadequate weapons and our poor Generals, we had been continually retreating, as were our allies and we seemed unable to turn the tide.

This frustration reached its absolute nadir in the winter of 1942. Just pause for a while and consider our situation. The Nazis had conquered huge tracts of territory in Russia, taking millions of prisoners with ease, whilst the spires of Moscow and Leningrad were in their sights. Rommel had taken all the ground we had previously won in Libya and was realistically within striking distance of Cairo. London was being bombed nightly, whilst German submarines were wreaking havoc with our Atlantic lifeline. The French were out of the war and appeared to be anti-British. To cap it all, the Japanese had all but wiped out the American Pacific Fleet at Pearl Harbour. Our Base at Singapore had capitulated, with the Royal Navy in that region being literally wiped out. We had been captured, and many of our comrades had died in North Africa. Meanwhile, there we were rotting in a God-forsaken spot in southern Italy.

Every week which went by in the camp saw some P.O.W. go 'round the bend', only to be carted away in a wooden contraption to some lousy Italian asylum. To stop our minds from rotting away and to keep our spirits up, we decided to organise a Discussion Group. It originally seemed a long shot as so few P.O.W.s were interested. It started with only a few hardy souls gathered around together, desperately trying to keep warm huddled in our blankets. Curiosity attracted a few more, until we announced a debate with a dynamic soul-searching title – "That Christianity has been more a force for evil than for good". In our present circumstances we were at a low ebb and some of us wanted to blame someone or something for our plight.

Some had seen terrible sights, having now experienced at first hand man's inhumanity to man, not having given much thought in the past to the whys and wherefores of life. For the first time in their lives they were faced with expressing their deeper thoughts. The motion was proposed by a Sergeant, who before the war had been a representative for the publishers Victor Gollancz, a well-known left-wing publisher. He was extremely fluent, being a Cambridge-educated man. The opposer was a Sergeant from Wales, who had been a lecturer at Cardiff University in Theological Studies.

The debate started at about 10.00 a.m. with around 100 men gathered around, and as time passed more and more joined in until there was a break for our midday soup. Word of the proceedings passed around to the four corners of the camp, until we had at least a thousand listening to the argument. The proposer waxed forth about the genocide committed by the Catholics in South America, similarly by the Protestants in North America. For good measure we were told of the sacking of Constantinople and Jerusalem by the Crusaders, and even of the tragic Children's Crusade. The opposer detailed how the early Christian churches had kept alive the culture and knowledge during the Dark Ages and stemmed the pagan hordes. There were a surprising number of questions asked and skilfully answered for quite a period of time.

At about mid-afternoon I took a vote by a show of hands and, believe it or not, there was a clear majority of about two-thirds in favour of the motion. After seeing man's inhumanity to man for so long, an overwhelming cynicism had taken hold of the men's minds and outlook. They had concentrated their thoughts in a way in which they would never have done in normal circumstances. To their embittered minds, religion had been thrown overboard. To be fair, when I asked their opinion many months later, when the Red Cross parcels had arrived and the Allies were winning battles at last, then their cynicism began to wane. I believe that if the same debate had been held in 1945 there would have been a different result. War concentrates people's minds on religion!

The two greatest problems facing us in the early days in Italy were bed bugs and lice. Initially, the bed bugs spread like wild fire. In the morning we would wake up with bite marks on our arms, legs and bodies. These bite marks were surrounded by swollen blobs of skin, which itched in a painful way until about midday. Many of my friends were woken up in the night by these painful predators but luckily, being a heavy sleeper, my problem did not become evident until I woke up. After daylight we would take our mattresses outside and lay them on the ground in the early morning sunlight.

We could see the bugs congregating in the mattress seams and would run our fingers along, levering them out. We would then squash them between two pieces of wood or sometimes tip them into an old tin and put them in the cookhouse fires. After that we would take the wooden bed laths outside to the edge of the cookhouse fires, where we would poke a stick in the fire, wait until the point of the stick was glowing, then run it along all the cracks in the wood. After this procedure, the bed laths would be a mass of scorch marks mixed with blobs of our blood, where we had scorched the lice as they crawled out of the cracks.

One optimistic soul decided that he would get tin lids from the Red Cross parcels, fill them with water and attach them to the bed legs, on the assumption that the bed bugs could not swim. However, when the bed bugs appeared again as usual, this Royal Engineers' man blithely stated, "I reckon I was right that they cannot swim, as they have crawled up the walls and dropped in from the ceiling."

From the Italian Quartermaster we requested we should be issued with a stock of paraffin as we felt that this would solve the problem, but all we got from our repeated requests was, "Dopo domani." So the paraffin never appeared. For months we battled on, burning them out or squashing them between our fingers to the embattled cry of, "Bastardo." Eventually, we had a reprieve when the Stove Wagon arrived. This was a contraption, which was wheeled into the camp, with steam at pressure, as we all stripped naked and pushed every item of clothing in. We closed the door, sat around and waited, and eventually recovered our clothing, which seemed to have shrunk by about two sizes. As not all the Huts were stoved, the whole exercise was only a temporary palliative in the ever-growing battle against both the bed bugs and – worse than ever – lice.

Yes, now we come to lice, which were a problem throughout our time in southern Italy, which were ameliorated in Northern Italy, and totally absent in the camps in Austria. In the first camp, No. 65, in southern Italy, they appeared very soon after our arrival and multiplied at great speed. They were present in every indentation in our clothes. We would sit around each morning in the sunshine, running our fingers down every seam, cracking them continuously until this became a mechanical daily procedure. I have described in a later chapter how we forced the Italians to delouse us after we craftily dropped lice on the Adjutant's uniform, thereby transferring our problems to them. Just another example of how we had become streetwise in order to survive. One of our mottoes had become 'needs must when the devil drives'.

I clearly recall the end of the first week at Camp 65 when, following the morning Roll Call, the Adjutant announced barbers would arrive and our wayward locks would be shorn. We were not allowed any razors or scissors, so we would all be forcibly shorn. This really pleased us as we were constantly rummaging through our unkempt hair, which was full of head lice. After some months of growth we looked like a motley collection of Rip Van Winkles.

On the appointed day we watched each other underneath the scissors (sometimes they felt like shear blades) to loud peals of laughter as each man stood up – there we were, entirely different now, heads completely shaven like a group of Chinamen. We were entirely white on top, while our faces were deep brown after all those months in the desert sun. One wit remarked that we were all now members of the 'Two Tone Brigade'. Also, after so long on short rations, we had a somewhat cadaverous appearance. After this scissor session we almost had difficulty in recognising each other. It's amazing what a difference a bald head makes. How fresh we suddenly felt and we recognised that we had all taken a step towards normality. The exceptions were some of the South Africans who had always sported the familiar Jan Smuts pointed beard. They were now a new distinctive group. At least it had proved a hilarious interlude – anything to break the monotony.

One day we were all issued with a simple card to fill in, stating that we were now in an official Italian Prisoner of War Camp, No. 65. We were in good health and could receive letters from home. Our spirits were lifted considerably at the thought of receiving letters from home. We were promised that we would be issued with a standard letter form by the Red Cross, so that we could write home each month. These letters would, of course, be censored. Before Christmas, great excitement ran through the Camp when letters arrived from home. I collected all the letters on the nominal roll of my Hut. As I read out each name to receive a letter, there was a wide range of emotions apparent as I moved amongst those who had not received one. I then had to try and cheer them up as far as possible. Several in my group were regular soldiers who were in India at the outbreak of war in the 4th Indian Division, and had initially been posted to the campaign in East Africa and then to the Western Desert. It would be many months before they received letters.

As the months went by, letters were shown to me by some who had received tragic news from home, such as deaths in the Blitz. It was also heart-breaking in some cases where wives had written to say they had fallen in love with someone else. I was now witnessing a whole range of human emotions, which were quite new to me. One young Cockney soldier said to me, "I love my wife, she is the whole world to me. I thought she was proud of me as a soldier, but now life offers me nothing." I lamely said, "Life has many ups and downs." He retired to his bunk and stared at the ceiling. At Roll Call the next morning his bunk-mate told me that he was still in bed staring at the ceiling. I didn't drag him out but reported him sick. He remained like this day after day. Eventually I hauled him out of his bunk, made him wash, and sat with him for a while, but received not the slightest reaction from him of any sort.

We had a Medical Officer who was based at an adjoining camp and I dropped him a note asking him to call and see this tragic case. In due course he arrived and made an examination. He said to me, "The shock of the letter has temporarily unhinged him. Excuse him all Roll Calls and move him into the Sick Bay." Several of us sat with him, spoon-feeding him and never getting a word out of him at all. Looking in at him one morning, I moved closer and saw that his skin had a waxen appearance. I felt his pulse. He was dead.

The Medical Officer confirmed his death, saying to me, "There you have a classical case of a man who has just simply decided to die. I can find nothing medically to prove why he died, but he has clearly died of a broken heart. This is a fact, but I cannot give this as a cause of death so it will be heart failure. Keep a close watch for we shall have more like this." And of course, we did. The Medical officer said, "Leave it to me and I will write to his widow." I handed her letter to him and he said, "Well, there is one female back home who will be pleased to receive my letter." We were now truly living in brutal times.

Another day of great excitement when battle dress blouses, trousers, shirts, underpants and boots arrived. The luxury to me was a pair of boots. My soft-soled desert boots, or Boots Patrol Mark 1, had given up the ghost a couple of months previously, the soles parting from the uppers. I had had to bind strips of cloth around them, which had been given to me by the Adjutant, who had taken pity on me one day when I walked behind him on Roll Call. My bound boots squelched on the Parade Ground and annoyed his musical senses.

When the first Christmas came, although it was cold and miserable (for it can be cold and miserable on the toe of Italy in winter), at least we now had warm clothing and dry feet. On writing this at my ripe old age, I realise how youthfully fit we all must have been to stand around for so long with our feet in such muddy conditions and also with so little clothing.

We were making progress. We had a new saying by now, "Survive the first three months and we can last forever". Making up the Nominal Roll at the end of one particular month, Sergeant Major Cameron casually said to me, "Winter, how many stiffs in your Hut this month?" To which I replied, "For the first time, I can report a nil return." Cameron's reply was, "Your lot must be battle hardened by now."

With a supply of Red Cross parcels arriving, containing new uniforms and especially new boots and socks, we were in seventh heaven. To keep fit we would stroll around the wire without a pause many times a day, still cursing the sight of barbed wire everywhere we looked. One morning Cameron addressed the Parade and said, "We are now getting food in our stomachs, so we shall begin to look like soldiers again. I have scrounged from the Italians some suitable strips of cardboard which will be placed under your mattresses at night, then you will dampen your trousers, neatly fold and place them between the cardboard and – hey presto – trousers in the morning with perfect creases.

The Italians were amazed to see us on Parade with perfect creases in our trousers, allied to which was exaggerated saluting and coming to attention etc. It was all part of our way of proving that we were still real soldiers and that we regarded them as a complete shower!

Of those who went round the bend in the early days, Sergeant Lander was among the most tragic. He was one of the men I most admired, with a sharply perceptive mind, but this was his undoing, as the life around him just became too much for him to handle. I put him in charge of one of the bays in my hut. There were about 300 men in six separate bays, and he was the N.C.O. in charge of Bay No. 1, containing about 50. At the outset, he was the perfect N.C.O., meticulous in trying to establish a degree of cleanliness, always working hard to raise the morale of his group. This was important in those early days when we were always battling with the gnawing pains of hunger and the lack of suitable clothing, which meant that it was hard to keep warm when the cold eastern winds swept across the bleak landscape, and, of course the ever present fleas, lice and bed bugs.

To compound this, no Red Cross parcels had arrived. We were a miserable lot.

Lander would spend many an hour with those who were suffering from severe depression. He had a knack of bolstering up spirits by talking them through situations. Having been a teacher in the West End of London, his cultured accent seemed to upset some of the Cockneys around him. He himself had suffered the experience of being a member of a tank crew in the thick of the battle of the Cauldron near Tobruk, where our tank losses were enormous. His squadron had been caught in murderous crossfire from 88mm guns dug in hull down (i.e. with only the gun barrel showing). His tank had received a direct hit and 'brewed up' (as we used to say when a tank caught fire). He was the only survivor.

The men in his Bay were a rough lot and I really ought to have transferred him. They had crude manners and did not appreciate his efforts to help them. Realising this, he himself became more and more depressed. Living in such close juxtaposition as P.O.W.s meant you could not avoid those who were louts. One evening there was a loud commotion in his Bay and I went to investigate. Two of the louts had been fighting and he had intervened and tried to break them up, when they had both turned on him, beating him up badly. He was lying in his bunk with blood streaming from his nose and both eyes almost closed. I bathed his face and stayed with him for a couple of hours. He kept uttering, "I can't stand this any more – this is the end."

The next morning one of his friends came up to me just after dawn asking me to come and look at him. There he was sitting cross-legged on his bunk, staring vacantly ahead and talking continuously without a pause of any kind. The whole gamut of his vast accumulated knowledge was pouring forth as he switched from maths to history to geography to art etc ad infinitum. I moved him into the bunk below me in my bay, reporting him sick, and for five days he talked and talked without a pause. In the end it was obvious that we could not do a thing to help him. The Medical Officer came to see him and reluctantly transferred him to the Italian Sick Room. I called to see him before they took him away. There he was sitting cross-legged, still talking and talking. I shudder to think that he may have finished the war in an Italian asylum.

In those early days fights were common, but not much real damage was done as men were too weak to batter each other too badly. When Red

Cross food parcels arrived, most of the old animosities were forgotten and friendships blossomed. All the problems caused due to the gnawing hunger pains became a memory. It was then that I realised one of the easiest ways to break a man's spirit is to deny him food. Until you have experienced the real pangs of hunger you cannot realise what an effect this has.

One evening I was strolling round the wire with Smudger Smith, a Cockney who always displayed an optimistic outlook on life and Stampy Stamper, a gunner from Newcastle who had a lively mind. His family owned a bookshop in Newcastle and it was obvious that he read most of the shop stock before he sold it. He stopped and said, "What about forming an Anti-Boredom Committee. We could call it the AB Committee." "No chance," I said, "We haven't even got an Escape Committee." "That's just it," he retorted, "No one is fit enough to escape and even if we did then these local peasants would kick us to death. We should try and raise the spirits of these lads by thinking up ways and means of playing tricks on the Eyeties (short for Italians). Surely that shouldn't be too hard." And so the idea was born.

All P.O.W. Camps were organised around a Camp Committee, so we first sought and obtained their approval, then planning began in earnest. The combined think tank went into action and our first venture was named 'Operation Lice Transfer'. If the Italians would not delouse us, then we would transfer the lice to the Italians. It was noticed that when they came into the camp they would keep a reasonable distance from us to avoid any involuntary transfer of lice. So this is what we did.

It was the 1st December 1942, a cold, muddy and miserable morning as we waited with bored attitudes, as usual, to be counted. There I was with water slowly seeping through my desert boots, and the longer we waited, the wetter my feet became. Eventually the Adjutant appeared, also looking bored as usual. We had long since nicknamed him the 'Corset King', being convinced that he wore corsets. His lovely blue uniform with gold edging fitted tightly around his waspish waist and seemed to be in tune with his haughty air of disdain towards us. Well, I suppose we did emanate a rather special odour at that time.

My state of mind was somewhat tempered by the thought that in my pocket was a small box of luscious swarming lice, which were destined for the body of the Corset King. He halted a respectable distance from me. I took one pace forward and saluted him smartly. The Sergeant interpreter detached himself and I followed behind him. On the second row we were hidden from the rest of the Italians and I slipped the half-open box around his neckband. He stopped and I just had time to adjust my distance when he said, "Why is everybody staring at me?" I replied that it was because they were all so impressed by his freshly pressed uniform. This pleased him and he carried on. At the end of the line I said that I had counted one more than the Sergeant, consequently Corset King flew into a rage. After uttering several 'sacramentos' in a loud voice he took charge to show his authority and began counting himself. This left the Sergeant behind. After shouting about an Italian fool and an English fool he stormed down the line followed by me, at one point close enough to empty the rest of my little friends on the back of his shoulders. The spirits of those who were able to watch this bit of jiggery-pokery soared immediately.

Now all we had to do was to wait just a few days until, not surprisingly, the Delousing Machine was trundled through the Main Gates to rousing cheers from ourselves.

From then onwards we had a veritable plethora of ideas surfacing for discussion. One of these ideas, which seemed particularly ridiculous, turned out to be the source of great amusement. A small group of Coldstream Guards, had been outside the Camp on a clearing up party and had found some odds and ends, which they picked up and hid in their uniforms. We always worked on the assumption that we might find a use for anything we found. They had found some thin strips of metal and a section of thick strong elastic. As we sat around wondering what could be done with this innocuous find, the suggestion came from one of them that we should mount 'Operation Peashooter'. The idea was to build a Peashooter with which to surreptitiously bombard the guards. After some skilful metalwork by R.E.M.E. craftsmen, a suitable tube with a smooth mouthpiece was made and the cookhouse staff supplied the ammunition – dried peas. A competition then ensued to find those with the greatest degree of puff and by a coincidence it was the Guardsman who had found the strips of metal tubing.

Then one morning a small group of P.O.W.s were taking their regular walk around the perimeter when the shooter levelled his tube on the shoulder of the outer man and puff – the guard who had been snoozing in his box suddenly jumped up with a cry. It was a bullseye!

We waited a couple of days before the next attack at the other end of the camp, and in the meantime we had decided what to do with the elastic. The success of the peashooter turned our minds towards something more ambitious – a super catapult! The elastic was so strong that our craftsmen decided that they had to build a very strong base. And they did. With the advantage of some angle iron and a couple of wing nuts (these were half inched from a workman's bag when he wasn't looking) it was decided to mount this device on the post of a wooden bed near to an opening window. In our primitive huts there was no glass, just openings here and there. Our infernal machine was positioned with a good angle of fire , but was designed to be speedily dismantled and hidden from the enemy. We tested the elastic, which was surprisingly strong and evidently capable of considerable range.

The next morning we did a test firing and it was eminently successful. We collected a pile of small stones and secured the wing nuts on the bed nearest the opening. When the elastic was pulled back the wooden bed creaked and groaned alarmingly and as the stone whizzed through the air we realised it would fall short. Two more tries, and on the third attempt the stone hit the donkey which brought supplies up to the camp daily in panniers. It let out a startled bellow and was transformed into a bucking bronco, scattering soldiers in all directions. We were highly delighted at this, but in view of the tremendous consternation caused we thought it would be politic to wait before launching a further fusillade.

Over the next few days we concentrated on pinging several sloppy soldiers walking around their compound, but the outstanding success came when we pinged the bucket of the local milk girl as she was passing. The pail was empty and it reverberated loudly. She was so shocked that she fell off her bike. However, one of our team pointed out that she had such a large bust, that she was inherently unstable at the best of times. However, given our record to date of some very successful shots, we decided to go for the big one. We would try and ping the Commandant's window. We had two shots and then moved the bed nearer the opening in our hut to give us just that extra range. Finally we hit it and with a crack the window was shattered.

As the old saying goes, 'pride goeth before a fall,' and it did, because a few days later when we lobbed a shot amongst a group of soldiers about to change guard, there was a hullabaloo and a squad suddenly rushed into the camp straight for the point from where we had fired. We found that the

Commandant had been sitting waiting with a pair of binoculars and the squad was a decoy. We could not hide our infernal machine in time so we were now in trouble. We had a moral victory which was tempered with the thought that he would get even with us. The water was off for a few days because of a plumbing fault and one of the guards slipped and let a block of rock salt land in the soup ready for our evening meal. But it was worth it.

We buried the hatchet for a while until the AB Committee came up with another idea. 'Corset King' had a habit of coming into the Camp when his men made a periodic inspection of the huts, and he would stand near the Main Gate looking important. It satisfied his ego to watch the P.O.W.s saluting him as they passed, for we maintained the highest military standards. His military conduct was also correct as he punctiliously returned all our salutes. This was his undoing. The AB Committee then instituted 'Operation right arm ready to drop off'. On Monday morning (everything seemed to happen on a Monday morning) I marched out of Hut 1, past 'Corset King', giving him a smart exaggerated salute, left wheel and round the corner. Ten yards behind me came the next man and ten yards behind him the next. Before the remainder of the 300 men had time to appear he dropped his weary arm and retreated in disorder. Though we had to admire him, he could take a hint! From then onwards we turned to more leisurely pursuits

I must mention two occasions when we had a brush with the Italians, remembering that we tried always to maintain a moral ascendancy over them, after all it was our only weapon. This was in the days before Red Cross parcels arrived. The morning Roll Call would drag on and we would stand there, some of us with a thin blanket drooped around our shoulders. As each group was counted, a line of guards would hold us back with fixed bayonets. When the Roll Call was completed, a whistle would blow, the guards would stand on one side, and we would all rush forward to huddle round the cookhouse, the warmest spot of all when the wood-burning stoves had just been lit. One of the guards, unlike most of the others, was about six feet tall and an obvious bully, and one day, after we broke ranks and rushed forward, he deliberately did not draw his rifle into the upright position and one of the troops ran into the bayonet, not able to stop because of the pressure from behind. We knew that the guard had kept the bayonet level.

He was kept off duty for several days then appeared one morning leering in his usual style. Cameron then immediately called the Hut Leaders together, "We can't let them get away with this," he said. A plan was then agreed for the next day that when the whistle blew we would make for the cookhouse and, as Cameron succinctly said, "We'll do him in." And we did. Nearly everyone was wearing desert boots (or Boots Patrol Mark 1). We then had to find two men from each hut who had the usual standard heavy army boots, so each hut leader went back to his hut and gathered his 300 men together to check on their boots. I said to mine, "The exercise tomorrow morning is to down him and those with boots will kick him to death or trample on him." I located two but one young soldier said, "I couldn't do that," so I said to him, "What size boots?" I then said, "I want a volunteer, size 8." I was nearly bowled over by volunteers. Scratch the surface of most men under similar circumstances and you usually find savagery. We were all convinced that we were right. I went back to Cameron and said, "No problem." "Good show," he replied, "I've organised two solid P.T.I.s who will floor him and then those with boots will go in and the whole exercise should be finished in 20 seconds."

And that is exactly what happened. As we looked back from the cookhouse we saw an inert bloodstained body being lifted up and carried off. There was a dense trail of blood showing where he had been carried away. Cameron was sent for immediately by the Commandant and of course expressed his sympathy for the unfortunate accident. The Commandant knew, we knew, and we had made it clear to the enemy that, although we were their prisoners, we were not to be trifled with.

On the second occasion we were at first delighted when we were issued with a sugar ration. Although it was beet sugar, it was very welcome to add to the bitter ersatz coffee which was issued to us. This had to be shared out between 300 men. I collected the ration each morning from the Quartermaster's Stores after it had been officially weighed in the presence of the Quartermaster – a young dandified character. After a few weeks we detected that the ration was slowly being reduced. It was so precious that each man could almost count the grains. We decided on reflection that the weigh scales in the Store had been tampered with. It was then decided that I would contest the accuracy of the scales and, anticipating the action the Italians would take against me, the whole Camp would show their support in a suitable manner.

The next morning when the weighing took place, I said in a loud voice, "These weigh scales have been tampered with." The Italian Quartermaster screamed in rage, "Are you doubting the word of an Italian officer and a gentleman?" "There's no such thing," I shouted back. At this I was marched out and thrown in the Cooler. But we had anticipated this and I sat listening to the ever-increasing din outside. This was from the troops rattling their spoons around their aluminium 'dixies'. It really was a glorious cacophony of sound. The Adjutant came in, so in compliance with proper military procedure, I stood up, gave him an exaggerated salute, smiling all the time (in the British Army this would be classed as silent insubordination or 'dumb insolence'). "The Commandant's orders are that you will be let out but sacramento, I will make you all pay for this." A few days later a group of we malcontents were shipped off to another camp, but we thought it would be a pleasant change as one can vegetate if left too long in one spot.

I would like to comment on food in a P.O.W. Camp. We had strong teeth in those days and we needed them to chew into the incredibly hard bread rolls. Sometimes we came across portions of chestnuts in them, but at least they had a pleasant nutty flavour. On Sundays we were treated to a 'meat stew', which we eventually identified as mule meat. This required constant chewing but at least it lasted a long time and gave the illusion that it was a long meal. The macaroni soup was filling if you drank it slowly, but we had a craving all the time for more salt.

Near the end of 1942 life became bleak, as we were constantly hungry and it was absolutely forbidden even to talk about food. Every day we would drift aimlessly round the wire discussing the daily newssheet posted up by the Italians. For me, what had been a shirt was just hanging off my back and my shorts were all ragged along the edges. Five months of this lousy diet had weakened our constitutions and reduced our confidence in ourselves. Herb coffee, pasta soup and a small roll of hard bread per day represented the minimum necessary to keep us alive. Red Cross parcels had not arrived at this time.

Sometimes we would change our little groups of five. It gave us variety. In my group at this time was myself, George, a dour character from Newcastle, Buster (nobody ever called him anything else because even on these low rations he never seemed to lose weight), Tom, from a village on the Scottish border, where he was a gamekeeper, and Max, a South African who was a Ranger from Kruger Park – he was a supremely self-confident man who had been a member of a South African Recce Unit which had been constantly roaming far and wide in the desert.

As we moved along the perimeter the conversation turned to the forthcoming Christmas. I was thinking about the gargantuan Christmas dinners described in Pickwick Papers but dare not mention it. Just then we saw a mongrel dog nosing around the edge of the wire. Jokingly, Max said, "Look at that animal. Do you realise that is a feast on four legs?" We looked at it now in a different light. Max continued, "If we could get it through the wire then there is a wonderful meal waiting for us." We looked at each other incredulously. "What, eat dog?" said Buster. "Why not?" said Max. "The French eat horse, sparrows and snails, so why not dog?" The other four of us began to turn this over in our minds. There was a silence as we crouched on our haunches and gazed through the wire hungrily at our prey. Suddenly, Buster got up and strode off angrily – the temptation was too great.

For half-an-hour the dog wandered around and then disappeared. But we had already made up our minds. The pangs of hunger had made the decision for us. I knew then that in later life I would never apply to extreme situations the old rules I had been brought up with. We were at rock bottom and determined to survive. After all, we had an expert in our midst. We christened the poor dog 'Musso', and believe it or not, that helped us to overcome our scruples. All our waking hours in the next few days were occupied in luring Musso through the wire. We had nothing else to do but think about our deadly intentions and we trusted dear old Max.

The chief controller of events now was Max, who regarded the rest of us as lay-about city gents. "First of all we make friends with Musso and then lure him through the wire. To gain his confidence we must provide him with food. The determining factor in the life of every animal is food. We must sacrifice a portion of our daily bread ration each day." We groaned at this but it was all part of the game. When a precious part of my bread went through the wire I watched hungrily as Musso wolfed it down.

By this time our joint planning swung into action. Firstly, we had to scrounge a solid piece of metal from the surplus empty cans around the Cookhouse, and Tom proceeded to make a knife with a wooden handle and string to secure it. Hours of sharpening with suitable stones fashioned it into a reasonable knife. I couldn't resist quoting from the motto of the Cutlers' Company of Sheffield attributed to Chaucer, "A Sheffield thwittle bar he in his hose." "But I don't have any hose," said Buster.

Max then displayed how to make a 'blower'. This was a contraption made out of tin, which blew air along a suitable tube to the base of a perforated tray, which would hold pieces of wood from our bed boards. The draught of air came from metal vanes turned by a circular piece of metal and string. A totally 'Heath Robinson' contraption, which was nonetheless very effective. In fact, after Max's sterling effort, many were made around the Camp. Not for cooking dog, but the contents of Red Cross parcels in the future. The vessel in which to cook the dog was made from a large surplus can from the Cookhouse. So now the equipment had been manufactured and all that remained was to lure and despatch the victim.

Tom was the number two practical man among us and he would move along the edge of the wire gathering dandelion and other weeds, always careful not to get too close to the edge of the wire, or else a shout would be heard, "Attenzioni." I was merely the labourer in all this, chipping slivers of wood from the bed boards for our fuel. Through all this, Buster adopted a very 'hands off' attitude, but we were sure that he would change his mind when the stew began to bubble.

That night I lay on top of my bunk, fully dressed as ever in my tatty shirt, covered in the thinnest blanket ever produced in an Italian factory, and thought of the pre-Christmas dinner to come. I dropped off to sleep dreaming of following Max across the veldt, shooting elephants and roasting great steaks on spits. I woke up suddenly to hear my stomach rumbling angrily.

Early next morning we trooped out of our hut and took up our stations again. Eventually Musso appeared. Four differently pitched 'come hither' dog whistles were sent in his direction. Then several scraps of bread began to drop nearby. Some scraps began to be pitched at a shorter range and with bated breath we watched our deadly efforts begin to succeed. Eventually we lured him through the last strand of wire.

I will draw a veil over the despatching of poor Musso. Suffice it to say that Max displayed consummate skill in the skinning. This I had never seen before, and we came to the conclusion that Max must have performed this task countless times. The cooking proceeded at a slow rate. The scene can be imagined. Five of us crouched around our home-made Blower, watching the contents in the cooking pan slowly simmering – the pieces of meat, and the green coloured mass of herbs and weeds which Max assured us were edible. Around us milled about a hundred P.O.W.s eagerly discussing the whole procedure. They watched as Max carefully divided the concoction into our aluminium dixies – five portions, for by now, Buster had joined in with us, proving that hunger can drive a man into dire straits. Each mouthful was delicious as we looked at the hungry faces looking down at us. In years gone by, we could never have envisaged this.

Final Days In Italy

A further joke we played on the Italians had us bursting our sides with laughter. When both the Commandant and the Adjutant suddenly began to be friendly with those in charge of the huts and those who had to frequent their office for the various administrative matters which cropped up, we became extremely suspicious of their intentions. As Quartermaster, I had to go to the office every morning to weigh and count the bread ration, which arrived daily in sacks. When the bread had been weighed, counted and placed into blankets, the hut leaders would then draw the ration for their hut. When this was completed we would chat to the Italians in our poor Italian and they would reply in their even worse English. We realised they were frequently asking us what our civilian occupations had been. We decided to confuse them by inventing fanciful occupations.

The Commandant called our Camp Leader, Sergeant Major Cameron, into his office one morning. "The Italian Government is making a survey of all British P.O.W.s," he said pompously. "I have received a batch of forms which I would like you to issue to every man, and see they fill in all the simple details we require." Cameron looked through them and the information required was: 'Name, Age, Technical Education, Occupation.' "But you do not have the authority to ask us for this information," Cameron said, and then "Under the Geneva Convention, all we are bound to declare is 'Name, Rank and Number,' and you already have this for each man." Cameron realised the Italians had an ulterior motive in their request. It seemed highly likely that they were going to try and recruit P.O.W.s with specialised skills to work in their armament factories.

How little the Italians knew the British! There was no chance of them getting a single volunteer to work for them. However, perhaps we could turn this crazy scheme to our advantage. Cameron said to the Commandant, "I shall have great difficulty in getting 2,000 men to fill in these forms without some inducement." "Such as?" said the Commandant. "Well," replied Cameron, "I reckon a double bread ration might do the trick." "Done," was the reply. "When you return the forms to my office, I will issue a double bread ration." "Oh no," corrected Cameron. "The extra bread ration will have to be issued beforehand to persuade the form fillers." Cameron returned and called a meeting of the six hut leaders. We sat around to devise a plan. It was agreed we would fill in the forms in order to get the extra bread ration, but it was up to each individual whether the occupation put on the form was true.

I filled in my form by stating that I was 'The Archbishop of Canterbury's Wand Holder'. Other 'occupations' put on forms were 'Glass Hammerer', 'Snow White's Personal Assistant', 'Knocker Up', 'Cowboy's Six Gun Polisher', 'Third Man on Shovel', 'Dodo Hunter's Arrow Manufacturer', 'Sikh's Elephant's Tusk Cover Polisher' and 'Zulu Chief's Assegai Manufacturer'. For educational backgrounds we had a pupil from 'Pentonville College' and a graduate of 'Wormwood Scrubs University'. Others had been educated at more Colleges and Universities of international repute. Sergeant Major Cameron decided he would not make the presentation of the forms to the Commandant as he would not be able to keep his face straight. He gave me the task, saying I was better at play-acting.

The next morning at Roll Call, and having received and eaten our extra bread ration, I solemnly strode forward and handed to the Commandant the pile of forms all duly filled in. "Grazie, grazie," he said and glanced through the first few forms which had been carefully sorted out by us. We waited in gleeful anticipation for his reactions. The Parade was silent. As the Officer read the first six forms, a puzzled look came to his face and the whole Parade burst into fits of laughter. Pandemonium reigned and the Commandant, his face a deep purple colour, went into a rage. He shouted, "You will all pay for this," and stormed out of the gate in humiliation. We had had the best laugh since being captured. The punishment received was that for several days we were kept standing long hours for Roll Call, with the Corporal counting us, then re-counting over and over again. We all showed our feelings with continuous peals of laughter running through the ranks.

After the form-filling episode, Cameron and I detected a positive attitude towards us by the Commandant. We were fully supported by the other N.C.O.s and W.O.s. Matters came to a head when one of the duty sergeants who was carrying the daily bucket of cookhouse swill, unfortunately stumbled while passing close to the Adjutant. His bucket overturned and some of the contents spattered over the Adjutant's beautiful blue-striped riding breeches.

The recipient of the next trick was, once again, the Adjutant. At Roll Call each morning he would lean against the wall of the Hut and watch the proceedings lazily. This was our cue, and after a week's work we were ready. We made a metal container, large enough to hold about half a gallon of water, from tins delivered in Red Cross parcels which had been discarded once their contents had been consumed. Using tools fashioned by our Royal Engineers and R.A.O.C. personnel, a hole was bored in the hut wall at a point above where the Adjutant normally stood, and we then made a pipe and attached it to the container. The end of the pipe was tailored to be slightly protruding from the wall and the other end had a lip section. One morning we gleefully contributed our share of urine into the container and carefully hoisted it up on to some brackets we had fixed on the inside of the wall. These were at the correct height to ensure there would be sufficient force of gravity to project our precious liquid in the right direction. One man reported sick to the Sergeant Major and remained in his bed at the far end of the hut. He would be checked individually before the Roll Call count began. The signal to him was that on a prolonged loud bout of coughing from the men on Parade, he was to slip out of bed and pull the plug out. We were far from pleased when, for the first time, the Adjutant stood in a different position that morning.

For three mornings running we waited for him to take up the right position. The problem was that the liquid in the container was gathering strength daily. We had almost decided to call it off when, to our great delight on the fourth morning, the Adjutant stood in the right position. Suddenly we were stricken by a heavy bout of coughing, the 'sick' man inside the hut took his cue, slipped out of bed and pulled the plug, and the Adjutant and his smart uniform received a sprinkling of urine which had, by that time, passed its sell-by date. The 'sick' man in the hut, having carried out his duty, nipped smartly back into bed, having first wrenched the brackets from the wall, put a plug in the incision we had made, dropped the pipe and container into a hole we had previously dug and swiftly covered it over. Outside, pandemonium reigned and the guards were bemused at what had seemingly appeared out of the blue. It enabled us to cover our tracks. For several days the Adjutant was 'in absentia'. When he did appear we passed him holding our noses. Later when we were in German hands, we realised that if we played tricks like that on them, they would willingly shoot at least one man as an example.

In later years I have realised that, during six testing years in the Army, I was at all times surrounded by much more humour than could be found in civilian life. The hard conditions of active service life bred a dry humour in any situation and the tougher the situation, the drier the humour.

The outcome of that and the other jokes played on the Italians was that fifty of us were transferred to another camp. We were marched down to the local railway station and loaded into cattle trucks attached to a passenger train. It turned out to be a very uncomfortable journey. Every time the train stopped there would be a clanging of the buffers and we would find ourselves in a heap at the front end of the truck.

We began to wonder how we could once again attain moral ascendancy over the Italians. As had frequently happened in the past, the opportunity arose. The train pulled into a small station on the Adriatic coast. We were allowed to get off a few at a time to use the 'tatty' toilet. As we walked across the station platform, we were eyed with curiosity by the locals, who no doubt were seeing British P.O.W.s for the first time. A number of them shouted abuse at us in Italian. As we were getting ready to jump back onto the truck, one of the Italians said in good English to Sergeant Johnson (the Glass Hammerer), "Where were you captured?" Johnson, with chest proudly stuck out, replied, "In Sicily, a few days ago." The Italian, looking dumbfounded, turned to his companions and translated in an excited flow of Italian. Utter confusion reigned amongst them, and as the train moved away we could hear an excited conversation and with much arm waving taking place.

Sergeant Major Cameron drily observed, "It was easy to get them worked up, wasn't it?" There had been signs of panic among the Italians when Johnson had mentioned Sicily, and they had believed it, although we knew the 8th Army was locked in deadly combat with the Germans in North Africa. The next few miles of the journey were spent devising a plan of action. We decided to wait until we reached a large station where the effect of our plan would be more pronounced.

We arrived at Ancona, a town on the Adriatic coast. Fortunately for us it was evening, and a time when the station platform was full of people going home from work. We were not allowed to get off the train to attend to the call of nature, as there were too many people about. We waited until the train started to move out of the station before carrying out our plan. As a number of us could now speak passable Italian we shouted out to the people looking towards us that we were captured British prisoners, paratroopers who had been dropped in Sicily, and there would be many more prisoners following.

The guards who were in the next carriage shouted out to them not to listen to us, as it was all lies. We in turn shouted what we had said was true, and we then heightened the tension by banging on the side of the truck singing, "Rule Britannia." As the train drew out of the station, we could see mass confusion among the Italians.

We realised that when we eventually reached our destination we would no doubt be received by an Italian welcoming party. We were correct and, arriving at Camp No. 73 at Modena near Bologna, we found the ambience here to be a great improvement on Camp No. 65. There is a great difference in all respects between the south of Italy and the north.

But first of all we had to pay for our mischievous behaviour en route from 65 to 73. On arrival we were lined up to be given a lecture and we were then counted. A few minutes later we were counted again, and again. The penance continued until the only thing we could do was to show a complete attitude of boredom, making the point that this was causing the Italians more hassle than they were causing us.

When we finally settled in at Modena we realised we had been sent to a much more comfortable and better-organised camp than the previous one. Red Cross parcels arrived regularly, one parcel per man per week. Halcyon days indeed! While letters from home were plentiful, the main downside in our lives was the news being received of the continued German successes in Russia. We found when talking to the Italian guards that they were very despondent at the heavy losses their forces were suffering on the Russian front. The whole Italian nation was becoming war weary.

To relieve the monotony of captivity we spent most daylight hours walking round the camp perimeter. Situated on the rich Lombardy plain it was pleasant to see lush pastures, paddy fields of rice and streams around us. The local peasants walking past the wire appeared to be friendly people, smiling and giving us sympathetic looks, especially the females, unlike the dour peasants around Camp No. 65. The local peasants here had fine acqualine features. They moved with a steady grace and the women – they were stunning!

We had been locked away from normal life for a year, and prior to being captured we had spent months in the Western Desert with not even a leave spent in Cairo. We now found ourselves in a land of pleasant people and handsome women. They knew it too and never hurried past our camp. We had plenty of time to stand and stare, our stomachs were full of real food thanks to the Red Cross parcels, allowing our long dormant imaginations to dwell on other matters.

The whole camp went berserk when one morning 'Latte' appeared on the scene. She was pedalling a bicycle with a milk pail attached to the handlebars, hence the nickname 'Latte' (Italian for milk). She proceeded from the far end of the camp and along the whole length, and became the centre of attraction for many days.

Dressed in a figure-hugging white dress with jet black hair flowing behind her, with large pendulous breasts swaying from side to side, she pedalled slowly along. To quote an old army phrase, she could 'bring the birds out of the trees'. In later 'civvy street' years when I saw film star Sophia Loren on the screen, I would remember Latte, the Italian siren.

The first morning she came past the wire there was a deathly silence, as every pair of ardent British eyes followed Latte's movements until she disappeared out of sight. Later that day word spread like wildfire round the camp about this exquisite apparition who had descended from heaven. The next morning hundreds of P.O.W.s rose out of bed early to take a morning stroll round the perimeter. This was unusual, as there were times when we had great difficulty in getting everyone out of bed in time for the morning Roll Call.

On time, a white-clad figure appeared in the distance pedalling along. The khaki-dressed figures strolling around the wire stopped. Hundreds of pairs of lusty eyes followed her until she disappeared between an outcrop of maize. As everyone trooped back to the huts I could hear their coarse and lewd comments and it was obvious what was in the minds of all those virile P.O.W.s. The following morning saw a repeat performance. This time the cry went up – "Latte, Latte, Latte." It was obvious from her flashing seductive smile she was enjoying the adulation.

On Sunday morning, much to the disappointment of the waiting throng, she did not appear. It was decided Latte must have gone to Mass. Monday morning dawned and the camp sprang to life again. By now Latte must have realised she was the cynosure of all eyes – all 2,000 pairs of them, even at 6.00 a.m. Gradually, as the days passed, her pedalling became slower. She would switch on her lovely pearly smile from passing the first strand of wire until she reached the last one. Low pitched, high pitched, and all tones of wolf whistles greeted and followed her every inch of the way. She would respond by ringing her bicycle bell and giving a little wave of the hand.

One day Sergeant Major Johnson, a tough hard-bitten regular soldier, who had served for many years in the 4th Indian Division, remarked as Latte went by, "One of these days she is going to wave that hard, she'll fall off her bike and finish up 'arse over tit', milk pail and all, and just imagine what that will mean – 2,000 blokes swarming over the wire to pick her up." The thought was fascinating. In the next few days we tried to encourage her, but her native Italian caution was clearly abreast of our intentions. She enjoyed the whole charade as much as we did.

One morning she jumped off her cycle to wheel it past the entire length of the wire. To everyone's delight, this doubled her appearance time. It was at this point that Sergeant Granelli, who had been an Ice Cream Merchant from Manchester, came into the picture. Although not our official interpreter, in spite of his name his knowledge of the Italian language was only average as he had lived in England all of his life. He was a handsome chap, the possessor of dark Neapolitan good looks, and that clinched it. Instead of merely shouting "Buongiorno" as most of us did, Granelli spoke to Latte in his best Italian, creating quite a good impression on her, so much so that she would walk level with him along the length of the wire. This also raised the level of our respect towards Granelli in the camp, where he basked in his new-found glory.

Latte chatted to Granelli as she wheeled her cycle along the length of the wire, with all the men following on. The sentries didn't seem to mind as, by this time in late 1943, the Italians had completely lost their belief in the war. After their chat, Granelli would stand at the end of the wire waving goodbye to Latte with an "Arrivederci," and would then relate to the others what they had said to each other – no doubt adding a few embellishments of his own.

One morning, by sheer coincidence, Granelli was standing with Sergeant Major Johnson when Latte rode into view. Johnson had his own version of the English language, every third word he spoke was an 'F' word. His entire conversation was sprinkled with Urdu, no doubt picked up during his Indian service. He also had that type of cunning, which comes naturally to a man who has had to look after himself in a hard world. Granelli and Johnson walked together, keeping pace with each other, and chatting to Latte. It was obvious that Sergeant Major Johnson was going to get in on the act, which would no doubt turn out to be very interesting and would liven things up.

Granelli interpreted what Latte was saying. "She says she loves to hear the Englishmen shouting 'Buongiorno' to her." "I'm not surprised at that," grunted Johnson, "I know what I would feel like if I cycled past a P.O.W. camp full of Italian birds every morning." "Yes, Sergeant Major, she says she would like to say 'Buongiorno' but in English." In a flash Johnson said to Granelli, "Tell her it's f... me." Granelli stopped dead in his tracks. "Oh no sir, I couldn't do that, it's not fair." "Do as you are told lad or I'll have your guts for garters." Granelli blanched, he was really a decent chap but, like the other troops, he feared the Sergeant Major. He therefore did exactly as he was told. Latte thanked him saying, "Grazie, grazie, tanto, grazie," and she was gone.

The following morning as the sun rose on the Camp at 6.00 a.m., all the 2,000 men were up and lining the wire. Even the cooks had left their precious stores unguarded. An embarrassed Granelli, whom we felt sorry for, stood well into the back row. Sergeant Major Johnson was standing at the front by the first strand of wire, with that ever-present cunning look in his eyes. He was going to thoroughly enjoy what was about to happen.

Latte appeared at the start of the wire to a pregnant silence. She dismounted from her cycle, flashed her seductive smile, and with a broad Italian accent shouted to all, "F... me," not once but all the way to the end of the wire. Back came the reply of, "Over here," from 2,000 lusty throats. Latte seemed to be puzzled that by merely saying "Good morning," she had made so many Englishmen happy.

For the next few weeks in which I stayed at this camp, there was a repeat performance by Latte every day of the week apart from Sunday when she went to Mass. The Sergeant Major said to me, "This is the finest tonic for getting troops out of bed I have ever known." "We British soldiers have a peculiar sense of humour," I said. Johnson replied, "I've always tried to spread a little British humour wherever I have been all over the world. Now it's Italy's turn." And I believed that in his own way he meant it.

It seemed strange that apart from Latte nothing very much happened in the months that we were incarcerated at Modena. Sheer boredom had taken hold until we decided to build an escape tunnel. Our tunnel was not to be the sophisticated one that everybody was later to read about in 'The Great Escape'. It was to be a hole in the ground stretching out and beyond the wire. The originator for this project was an ex-miner, 'Taffy', who, unsurprisingly, was from Wales. Having been a pit Deputy, he was put in charge. I was happy to play my part, until one particular day I was faced with an alarming situation. I was working my shift, stripped off, lying full length, digging away and putting the soil into a cloth bag. I would then give the string a tug and it would be dragged back.

As long as I could see daylight I was happy. Coming up against a large sewer pipe, we realised we could not tunnel over it as it was too near the surface, so we went under it and then continued at our original level. I looked back and not a ray of daylight could be seen. I hadn't the guts to tell the others that I was scared to work without seeing daylight, so I continued to dig away until there was a slithering sound and the tiny light on the wick in the olive oil lamp near my shoulder flickered. In a panic I grabbed the rope and it would not move. There had been a fall of earth somewhere near to the sewer pipe. My heart skipped a beat and I froze with fear. I began to dig furiously at the earth until I realised I must be using up all the air in my small space. The worst part was just lying down, doing nothing and waiting. Because of my strenuous efforts, sweat was pouring out of me. This was more frightening than the horrors of Dunkirk. I could hear the others working hard to clear the fall. It must have been only a few minutes before they reached me, but every minute seemed like an hour. Suddenly there was a most welcome draught of cool air. A very scared and sweat-covered Albert crawled to safety. The outcome was that I was excused from further digging.

As the days went by our conversations with the guards became more intense, and the Italians were clearly getting increasingly nervous, especially when a squad of heavily armed Germans arrived and took up positions overlooking the camp. We went to our bunks that night full of trepidation. The next day there was great excitement when a wireless announcement stated that, "Italy has sued for peace." For them the War was over, at least the fighting – or so they thought. The Germans moved down from their lofty positions and completely surrounded the camp. To our dismay they erected Spandau machine gun posts at each corner. The Italians just vanished. We then realised we had exchanged one lot of captors for another. At a number of Italian P.O.W. camps, the prisoners just walked out. Sadly, that was not to be our fate.

In German Hands And Moving To Austria

We were soon informed that our new German guards were members of the Marine Corps, but later found out they were some of General Kesselring's crack troops. They were commanded by a certain Oberleutnant Von Cramm, who in pre-war years had been famous as a tennis player. We were told that Von Cramm had said that, as a sportsman, he respected the right of any prisoner who wished to attempt to escape, but his men were under orders to shoot to kill if they saw anyone doing so.

That sobered us up.

A few days later we were given orders to gather our equipment, or what little we had, and to be ready to move off to a camp in Germany. Clutching our few possessions, we were marched out of the camp to Modena railway station, destined for an uncertain future in Germany. We were leaving the best Italian P.O.W. camp we had been confined in. As we passed through a suburb of Modena, we were astonished to see lines of local women with tears streaming down their faces. They threw bread rolls to us, which we gratefully accepted, thinking that a year ago we had been reviled and spat upon by the women of Brindisi. Once again, the fortunes of war. That is the philosophical thread that runs through the whole of this narrative of mine.

We marched through the streets of Modena in lines of three, trying to present as military a spectacle as possible, to impress both the Germans and Italians. Suddenly there was a wail of air raid sirens, creating such pandemonium as only the Italians can display. A large force of American bombers passed overhead, flying quite low. This had the Italians rushing to the air raid shelters praying to every Saint and Pope they could think of. Our pace quickened as the guards, sensing trouble, tightened the columns with roaring voices and waved their rifle butts as the sound of aircraft engines grew louder and louder. We thought at this stage we could be on the receiving end of about a hundred American Flying Fortresses. However, they had other plans. But it did make us wonder if we were about to finish our army careers in little bits and pieces on a street corner in Italy.

Then an incident occurred which seemed to have come straight out of a Hollywood movie. Marching directly in front of me was Sergeant Bristow, an ex-London docker, who, as he said, had "joined up to get away from those bloody awful docks." I saw the door of a nearby house suddenly open and a woman stood beckoning to Bristow. One second he was in front of me and the next second he was diving headlong through the open door, the woman stepping aside to let him in. I continued to be carried along on a moving tide of humanity.

Some time later, when we were northbound in a cattle truck, Bristow told me of what had happened after he had dived through the woman's door. The woman pointed upstairs, Bristow dashed up the narrow staircase, into a bedroom and crawled under a bed. A few seconds later a burly German soldier pounded up the staircase and into the bedroom, kicking with his jackboots at Bristow's boots which were protruding from under the bed. "Komm, Engländer," was the German's command, and out came Bristow. Glancing back he could see the German attacking the woman with the butt of his rifle.

"It just shows," he said, "It is really a case of hard luck. Just think what I could have done for the poor woman. I might have remained in that bedroom until the end of the war." Instead, he had been pushed down the stairs and out through the front door to join the tail end of the column.

We were loaded into a special train of about thirty cattle trucks – forty men to each truck. Sentry boxes were fitted on the top of the trucks at regular intervals. It proved to be an uncomfortable journey. Barbed wire was stretched along the apertures but we were able to see where we were going. Pat Jones, a tough regular soldier, found a pickaxe head, which had been left in a strategic spot by a friendly Italian railway worker. He stuffed it down his battle dress blouse as we crowded round to get into the same truck.

It was now all down to a matter of timing. The train was travelling at a fast speed. We thought that when it reached the foothills of the Alps it would slow down, but at the same time make more noise, as it laboured ever uphill. We would then be able to hack away and make a hole in the floor. A pack of cards was brought out and each man took one. The Ace card would be the highest and whoever drew that card would have the first chance of getting away. I drew No. 15.

The train slowed down as it approached the Alps and, as we hoped, became increasingly noisy as it went through a cutting. We worked furiously in relays cutting through the wooden floor, which was rotten.

Eventually a hole was made wide enough for men to drop out. The lookout said, "Hold on, there's a steeper grade ahead." We crouched round the hole watching the track beneath sliding by ever more slowly. It was agreed we would drop out with our legs apart to get a better balance, then roll forwards, but not move away until the train was well past, so the guards would not see us. By now it was almost dusk.

Then, to our disappointment, the train slowed down and finally came to a halt. We waited tensely, expecting our laborious efforts would be discovered. Then came the sound of marching boots, the door was unbolted and flung open, then harsh-sounding voices, "Ausgehen, schnell, schnell." We were informed that it was a comfort stop. Having been travelling for many hours, this stop was as important to the Germans as it was to us. Stretching out our limbs, we saw we were covered with a yellow dust, as the train had previously been carrying sacks of sulphur.

We had already covered the hole with broken timber to prevent it being discovered. As we lined up by the side of the truck, caustic comments came from the German guards about us looking like a patrol of Mongolians. I was standing behind a tall bush with guards to the left and right of me, all looking in different directions. Crouching low, I began to move away, coming to a halt when I found myself looking straight into the barrel of a Schmeisser gun. The German holding it grinned at me, saying in perfect English, "Get back Chink."

Back on the train, a clanging of doors, clouds of steam and a bellowing of oaths, and the train moved off. I peered through the aperture at the side of the truck and could see we were snaking round bends with tunnels looming ahead and mountains frowning down on us. The fatigue party was putting the finishing touches to the hole, to make sure there were no odd pieces sticking out preventing us from making a clean drop. Then followed a unique display of discipline. We all lined up behind Pat, with our numbered playing cards at the ready. Then came final instructions from Pat, "Drop down dead straight, roll into a ball, lie 'doggo' for a few minutes, then rush off to meet those lovely Italian birds. If you don't drop dead straight the wheel will go over you, but do not worry as, when they bury your bits, they'll identify you from the little plastic bits round your neck. You will then be recommended for the D.C.M." With those words of wisdom, he disappeared in a flash. Then No. 2 followed quickly, then No. 3 and No. 4 and others. I looked along the queue at the remainder. Some grinned, some looked apprehensive, others showed no emotion.

After being cooped up with the men for such a long time, I pondered on which of us would make it and who would not. The hard-bitten regulars and the loners seemed the most likely to succeed. Sergeant Major Johnson would sink a knife into the back of any German or Italian who got in his way, without batting an eyelid, while Sergeant Ward would not get very far unless he had a companion to show him the way.

Closer and closer I shuffled towards the hole. I was almost mesmerised watching, as bodies disappeared through it. Suddenly, there was a most unholy racket. Several machine guns opened up as the train screeched to a halt. Loud German voices could be heard against the crunch of boots on gravel. Then came the sound of truck doors being slewed open. Those of us left were frantically putting pieces of wood back covering the hole. We checked that twelve of our comrades had gone.

The door of the truck was pushed open and a German Sergeant Major strode in. Shouting and cursing at the top of his voice he counted us. Realising twelve were missing he went berserk, yelling, "Come out, one man to be shot." At this deadly command we crowded into the far corner of the truck. The German lunged forward and grabbed the smallest man amongst us, a Sergeant always referred to as 'Tanky'. He had been in many of the tank battles in the Western Desert and was badly wounded in the Battle of Sidi Rezegh. As a consequence, Tanky was always slow off the mark. If he had been able to drop out, I do not think he would have made it. We were horrified to see Tanky had been dragged out. We shouted at the top of our voices to the German and loudly hammered on the side of the truck. We could only watch in horror at the macabre scene which then took place. I could feel a line of blood running down my neck from a rifle blow to my head. But I was lucky compared to Tanky.

It was now dark. Two small searchlights had been mounted on the top of the trucks and were trained on Tanky. As his executioner pulled out his Luger pistol, Tanky begged, "No, no, don't shoot." "Turn round," raged the Sergeant Major and swung Tanky round, placing the revolver against his neck. The whole trainload of P.O.W.s were stamping their feet and shouting. The Sergeant Major turned round towards the din and shouted abuse at us. As he turned back to Tanky to administer the coup-de-grâce, the tall figure of a German Officer appeared, striding quickly forwards. He had been organising a sweep search down the track for the escapers, but on hearing the commotion had returned to the train.

A silence fell as we saw Tanky drop on his knees and pull out of his pocket a photograph of his wife and two small children, pleading desperately to the Officer for his life. The Officer said something to Tanky which we could not hear. Tanky returned the photograph to his pocket and sprinted back to join us. Before the train moved off, the Officer said to us all, "When we reach our destination, I will come along and inspect the truck personally. If there is a single man missing, then the Sergeant Major will shoot the lot of you."

When Tanky had recovered his breath, he told us that he had kept repeating to the German Officer, "Wife and two children. Wife and two children," and it had worked. He then said, "I'm a good Trade Unionist, but if anybody passes any derogatory remarks about the German officer class, I'll punch them on the nose."

After the 'Come out one man and be shot' incident, we sat down and looked occasionally at the hole we had made in the floor of the railway truck taking us to Germany. The thought of every man was, "What lies ahead for us?" As dawn broke, I looked out of the aperture at the side of the wagon and realised that, with mountains all around, we were in the lower Alps and moving through Austria. The scenery was magnificent, with clean pine-scented air floating into the truck. Someone remarked, "I hope they drop us off in Austria, that will be better than bloody Prussia." "Yes," another commented, "but remember that murderer, Adolf Hitler, is an Austrian, and the Austrians are totally committed Nazis, so what is the difference?"

Eventually, the train clanked to a halt at a small station, from where rows of wooden huts surrounded by barbed wire could be seen. A comment made was, "That barbed wire looks taller and thicker than the barbed wire in Italy." I replied, "Yes, and look at those strong watchtowers all around."

In Austria

Our experience over the last year meant we were quite experts at judging barbed wire. Every day while in Italy we had gazed at it and it had been impossible to push it out of our minds. Here we noticed a number of civilians moving around inside the wire. It became obvious that this place was a General Transit Camp. A camp for 'odds and sods'. When we saw a number of S.S. troops we began to feel uneasy. What had we come to? We were soon to find out and it was not to be very pleasant.

As we were hustled through the gate to be lined up outside the Commandatura, the guards were shouting at the top of their voices. Out of his office came striding the Commandant, also shouting at the top of his voice. (All orders were expressed at the highest decibel level the person was capable of producing). "You are now at Markt Pongau Transit Camp. If you behave yourselves you will eventually be sent to a recognised British P.O.W. Camp. Tonight a whistle will blow and you will immediately go to your allocated hut to be locked in. When the whistle blows in the morning, the doors will be unlocked and you will be free to walk around the camp. You must now obey orders, for in the German army we say, "Befehl ist Befehl (orders are orders*)* and you will be heavily punished if you do not do exactly as you are told." We knew that we were no longer in Italy and life here was going to be vastly different.

We were then directed to specific huts and noticed that we were being kept apart from the civilians. Dropping our kit on the two-tiered bunks, we decided to make a recce of our new home, trusting that we would not be remaining here very long. The hundreds of civilians we saw moving around had gaunt, non-smiling faces. They did not appear to be very well fed. We realised how fortunate we were to be wearing a recognised uniform, giving us some protection through the International Red Cross.

Among the civilians in the camp were many nationalities: French, Italians, Poles and Czechs, but no Russians. Some appeared to know why they were there, others were quite puzzled. Possibly they were hostages – a German procedure to terrorise civilian populations all over German-occupied Europe. We asked if there were any Jews because, while in Italy, we had been told that in every country occupied by the Nazis, the Jews had been savagely treated. Beyond our barbed wire was another fence with thicker barbed wire where two huts could be seen. Through the windows, women wearing headscarves could be seen making garments. A

Frenchman who spoke good English told us the women worked all day and every day of the week. The horrible thought occurred to us that these women were being worked to death. The Frenchman then said, "Aren't you lucky that you wear a British uniform?"

Early that evening we heard the whistles blow and a panic spread amongst the civilians who were walking around. They rushed past frantically, pushing us to one side to get to the doors of their respective huts. We said, "What a shower, we are going to march in step to our huts and demonstrate British discipline." Having marched only a few paces, we heard the baying of dogs. Looking round we saw a dog handler coming through the gates with a pack of fierce German shepherd dogs. He released them and they made straight for us. Our military discipline was completely forgotten as we dashed 'hell for leather' to our hut doors. Panting breathlessly, we dived in through the door, closing it with a bang. Safely inside, we could hear the dogs jumping up at the door, which was shaking on its hinges. It was the first time any of us had been attacked by such fierce dogs. We had thought dogs were 'man's best friend', to stroke and pat. That night we went to sleep feeling very uneasy.

On our recce of the camp we had discovered that in our compound, which housed several hundred prisoners, there was a single water standpipe in the middle of what we were to call the Barrack Square. Having survived our long journey from Italy, we decided to have a sluice down in the cold water that came down from the mountains. We had to get rid of the yellow sulphur dust we had collected on the train.

The following morning we were standing by the open window of the hut waiting for the guard's whistle to blow. Our determined intentions were to be at the head of the queue. After the whistle blew we sprinted to the standpipe, but there was a sudden loud clatter of machine gun fire. The guard in the watchtower, for some reason known only to him, had opened fire on us. In a panic we raced back to the hut. Fortunately he had fired only one burst, but one of our party had been hit and left lying on the ground. Back in the hut we banged on the walls and shouted, creating as much noise as we could. After a few minutes a Sergeant Major appeared and the wounded man was taken away. We later understood that when he recovered he was transferred to another camp.

After one more day at Markt Pongau we were dispersed to various P.O.W. camps in Austria. We decided the Germans were routing prisoners through this camp, so that when they arrived at an established British P.O.W. camp, they would be able to describe as newcomers what a Transit Camp was like, possibly to deter escapees.

With recollections of my past internment in Italy, here are some personal comments about the Italians. When they appeared to be winning the war (or so it seemed at the time), we would make them pause and see how we British kept our discipline in the face of hardships. We mocked them and played tricks on them. We could see that their hearts were not in this war as ours were. Eventually, they believed that, by making a separate peace, they could just opt out. What they didn't take into account was that there was already a large German army of experienced and ruthlessly trained troops positioned throughout Italy. Hitler was furious at their weakness and treated them with contempt and without mercy, even though many Italian Fascists still supported the Nazis.

Italy suffered enormous material damage from Allied bombing and the savage German reprisals taken against the civilian population. Here is a quotation from a declaration made to all serving German forces in Italy. These orders, signed by Field Marshall Kesselring, were issued in July 1944 as the Allies were pushing forward on all fronts.

1. Captured partisans are not prisoners of war and will be shot on the spot.
2. Civilians will also be shot who:
    (a) Supply partisans with food, shelter and military information;
    (b) Commit hostile acts of any kind against the German Armed Forces.
3. Where partisans operate in large numbers, hostages are to be taken from the population of the district in which they appear. In the case of brutal attacks, these men will be shot.
4. If soldiers and others are shot at from any locality, the village will be burnt to the ground.
5. Culprits or leaders will be hanged in public.
6. Orders for the burning of villages and individual buildings can be given by officers down to, and including, Battalion Commanders.
7. All civilians captured in battles with partisans, and in the course of reprisals, will be sent to collecting centres for transfer to the Reich as labourers.

To quote a further order given in August 1944 by the Commander of the 118 Grenadier Regiment, 'When the actual culprits cannot be found, hostages will be taken and an appropriate number will be shot, or hanged. In such cases, the whole population will be assembled to witness the execution. After the bodies have been left hanging for twelve hours, the public will be ordered to bury them without ceremony and without the assistance of any priest'.

When we were at Stalag 18a, we learned that there had been an armed fight between German troops and partisans at Tarvisio, near Udine. Thirty-two civilians, including women and children who had had no connection with the partisans, were machine gunned to death.

It was common knowledge in 1944 that the S.S. would shoot ten Italians of any sex for every German casualty. In an attack on an S.S. truck in Rome, when thirty Germans were killed, a round-up of local Italians – men and women, plus communist prisoners taken from a Rome jail – was carried out. They were put into trucks and driven into the open countryside outside Rome. An S.S. squad found a large cave and forced the hostages into it. They were all shot – a total of 330. The cave entrance was dynamited and the massacre only discovered later when a shepherd boy noticed swarms of flies coming out of a hole in the ground. The bodies were recovered for a sad identification and burial to take place.

Those who never left the shores of the United Kingdom during World War II are not usually cognisant of the savage barbarity that took place in any country occupied by the German army. I have found in conversation over the years, that people appear to have little knowledge of the many thousands of Italian citizens who had committed no crime whatsoever, but who were murdered as hostages.

We were very happy when told that we were to be moved to a Kriegsgefänger (British P.O.W. Camp). The night before leaving we had our last walk round the compound at Markt Pongau Transit Camp. We spoke to civilians from France, Italy and Yugoslavia. We felt sorry for them, especially the ones who had been grabbed from the streets of their home towns and, with nothing apart from the clothes they were wearing, had been thrown into cattle trucks and transported to this camp. In a confused state they were now awaiting their fate. These unfortunate people were innocent victims of the terror raging through Europe at the time. I have wondered over the years about how many of them finished up in

Dachau or some similar hellhole, suffering a slow death of lingering starvation or a quick death from execution.

I discovered it to be a small world a few years ago, when my wife and I visited Austria on holiday. We stopped for coffee at a small café in a village and were served by the café owner's son. He detected my poor speaking of the German language with an Austrian accent and I told him that during World War II I had spent a period as a P.O.W. at Markt Pongau, a few kilometres away. With a surprised look he asked me, "Were you there as an Englishman? My father has told me many harrowing tales about all the poor people who passed through that camp." I told him I had been a British P.O.W., but was only there a few days. I also said to him that I was pleased to know that the local people had not swept those memories under the carpet over the years, and that his father had taken the trouble to acquaint his son of the true facts, unpleasant though they were. Unfortunately, as his father was away I did not have the opportunity to speak to him.

We arrived at Stalag 18a, near Villach in South East Austria, towards the end of 1943. It was a comfortable and well-run Camp. We were given the facilities to organise many things. In addition to playing the violin in the Camp Orchestra, I also ran a gymnasium, held daily in a spare hut. It became very popular with most of the men, as a means of keeping fit and breaking the boredom of everyday life.

Fig: 22. Our group of 'keep fit fanatics' after an open-air workout during 1943.

In the winter of 1943/44, having read every book I could lay my hands on (some I had read twice), I decided to organise a library. I wrote to the Bodleian Library at Oxford, appealing for books on any kind of subject. To back this up I wrote to Professor J. D. Jones, Head of English at Sheffield University. Before the war I had become acquainted with Professor Jones through attending his Workers' Educational Association English Literature classes. He had nominated me for Ruskin College. The Professor and myself had kept up a correspondence in the various P.O.W. Camps in which I had been.

During our correspondence I asked him for his assistance by writing to any contacts he may have at Oxford and appealing for books for us. This proved very successful when, through the Swiss Red Cross, I received two large crates of books. I discarded the P.T. classes and concentrated on building up the Library. I obtained from the Camp Commandant a suitable supply of wood for shelves and I also received a great deal of welcome advice from a committee consisting of ex-university men, who helped me in installing a detailed library system. Highly delighted with my achievement, I appointed myself as the Librarian. I was enrolled in the University of Life where I could read all day and all night. In addition, any queries I had could be answered by ex-academics, qualified to answer my questions. Professor Jones sent me a list of books he recommended and I found this invaluable.

I took every opportunity to talk to the German Camp staff, some of whom were willing to talk of their experiences, especially those who had fought on the Russian front. Having been wounded, they had returned to be posted to P.O.W. camp duties. One told me a chilling story about life on the Finnish front and of the bitterly cold conditions there. The Finns appealed to the Germans to help them stem the tide of Russian attacks on their country. He said the temperature in that region was minus 40 degrees Celsius. As each side was well dug in, the only real activity was night patrols.

He told me of how one night he was ordered to take a patrol of 10 men and capture some Russians for interrogation. In the darkness, and wearing their white camouflaged suits, they moved silently forward over the snow-covered ground. They clashed with a Russian patrol carrying out the same exercise. After a short fierce fight had taken place, and having suffered only one casualty, both sides decided to return to their lines.

Much to the Germans' surprise, there came from across the frozen wastes, a voice booming out in German from a megaphone, "You have captured our Lieut Blenchov and we want him back. We have one of your men captive and we will exchange him." The Germans could find no trace of having the Russian officer and replied, "We can find no trace of capturing one of your men by our patrol." The Russians insisted the Germans were lying and if Lieut Blenchov was not returned, their German captive would suffer. Further conversations took place but, as far as the Russians were concerned, the Germans had their officer. He must have been a very popular man. The Germans insisted to the Russians that Lieut Blenchov's body must still be lying in the spot where the patrols had clashed. The Russians refused to accept this. Suddenly, a piercing scream rang out through the hard winter air. The Germans' blood ran cold, knowing it was leading to a cruel end for their comrade. The screams became louder and louder until they died out. It took half an hour for him to die. The German guard said to me, "Terrible people these Russians, terrible people." Participants in the savagery of war only have one point of view – their own. If I had said to the German, "You started the war and your country has displayed terrible savagery to the Russians," he would no doubt have said that they were only obeying orders.

We were impressed by life at Stalag 18a. There was a main camp and several smaller ones spread over a wide area. It was situated close to the town of Spittal an der Drau, the river Drau being a tributary of the River Danube. Nearby were the borders of Italy and Yugoslavia. As a consequence of the proximity of the uppermost area of Slovenia, we became interested and knowledgeable about the complications of the artificial State of Yugoslavia. The Slovenes and the Croatians were principally pro-German. Until after the First World War they had been part of the Austro-Hungarian Empire. Some of the people I spoke to, who were of my age group, had all been German speakers from birth, but when they became incorporated into Yugoslavia had had to learn Serbo-Croat. During 1943 the Germans recruited 15,000 volunteers, forming a complete S.S. Division – all Slovenes.

A half-bred Croatian named Tito Broz, but whose political name became Tito, was leading Serbian Communists against the Germans. This whole region became a veritable melting pot when the dénouement came at the end of the war – it became the night of the long knives. In 1945 many Slovenes and Croatians became displaced persons, having fled to Austria, from where many eventually emigrated to Australia.

Surrounded by this international grouping we had plenty to learn and occupy our minds. The camp was very efficiently run, with good discipline the order of the day. Mail and parcels arrived steadily. As Librarian, I organised discussion groups on all sorts of topics and subjects, so the days passed quickly.

Into 1944, we were becoming optimistic of an Allied victory. We had learned that a second front had been opened. The Adjutant of the camp, who came from Prussia, became more human and I had opportunities to talk to him. The old German arrogance was disappearing as I became more conversant with a view of German life outside the camp.

One day in 1944, I was with a group of others doing our daily 'trekaround' the perimeter of the camp, trying to keep fit, when we noticed a large Mercedes staff car pull up outside the Commandant's office. Shortly after this, our Camp Leader was sent for. On his return he told us that the visitor was none other than the famous Luftwaffe General, Kurt Student. Student had commanded the German paratroops during the invasion of Crete and when he saw that ours was a British PoW camp, he asked to speak to any British or New Zealand troops held there. I was given the job of searching out any such men.

I eventually rounded up a dozen men, including the inevitable 'awkward squad' character who thought it was all just propaganda, but even he tagged along in the end.

When we entered the Commandant's office, we were faced with a heavily be-medalled officer who immediately saluted us while grinning broadly. He told us that he wished to shake hands with the men who had opposed his paratroops in Crete. He added that the battle was a very close run thing and that the German losses were very high indeed. He considered himself nothing more than a professional soldier and professed his admiration for a gallant enemy, comprised of many part-time soldiers. We warmed to him.

Years later when I studied the German accounts of the battle for Crete, they bore out what he had said, and in fact the German paratroops were never used in that capacity again, serving only as a special infantry division.

He shook hands with all of us and said that he saluted us for our grim determination, but Krieg is Krieg (*war is war*). As we left the Commandant's office, I heard Student saying that his visit must be 'strictly confidential.

Later when we discussed the event among ourselves, we felt that this meeting really pointed out the futility of war, when such men can meet and converse without propaganda coming between us.

As the fighting in Italy began to move north, new prisoners were arriving at the camp who had been captured in Italy. We were beginning to get a much clearer idea of the progress of the Allied forces.

Early on a warm pleasant evening in September 1944, at the end of another monotonous day, we were walking round the camp perimeter. A goods train pulling cattle trucks was slowly making its way along the railway line that ran past the camp. We stopped to watch it. Dusk was falling, making it too late for Allied air attacks on the railway system. The signal was at red and the train came to a halt. From where we stood we could look into the trucks. Loud wailing from women could be heard, followed by desperate Italian voices. Many amongst us who could speak passable Italian shouted back. We then heard the tragic story from the women. They were civilians from an Italian village north of Venice, where there had been a Partisan attack on a group of German S.S. soldiers. The S.S. had carried out their reprisal orders – ten Italians for every S.S. casualty. With no Italian men around at the time, the S.S. dragged women off the streets or out of their houses. Herded into the cattle trucks, they had been without food or water for two days and were desperate. We were unable to help them and knew they were being taken to a camp called Dachau, near Munich. We remembered the German warning, "Watch yourself or you will finish up the flue." We had heard this several times, without realising the full horror of what went on in the extermination camps.

The following morning, when collecting the hut's rations, I said to Captain Kreiger, "Did you hear those poor Italian women being treated like cattle to the slaughter when that train stopped outside the camp?" He replied, "I was listening to the wireless." "Don't tell me that, you must have heard the wailing," I said. Kreiger, who had been badly wounded on the Russian front was, in civilian life, an Austrian landowner. I continued to have a go at him, "Come on, tell me the truth." He looked at me thoughtfully and slowly said, "The world will never forgive us for this." He knew, and we knew, it was only a one-way ticket to the concentration camps. We were all horrified by what we now realised was simply brutal murder being carried out on a large scale. We soberly reflected on what would happen to us if any of the secret weapons the Germans were always boasting about in their newspapers were used successfully, giving them victory in the war.

Talking to some of our guards, it was clear they were unhappy about the situation, but they had an underlying fear of what would happen if anyone stepped out of line. I was to see a clear indication of this when I suffered agonising pain from a bad tooth. The Commandant made arrangements for a guard to take me to the dentist in the nearby village.

The guard taking me was not a very bright young man. It was obviously the reason he was on guard duty at a P.O.W. camp and not fighting at the front. Having lived in the village all his life, he had a girlfriend who worked in a café which we had to pass on our way to the dentist. The dentist was an elderly man who spoke passable English. He extracted my painful tooth, and before leaving I shook his hand, thanking him. He said to me, "What a tragedy we are fighting England. It should never have come to this." It was obvious he had not been instilled with Nazi ideology. I commented to him that I had spoken to some of his countrymen who would not accept the view that the aggression had started from their side until I pointed out that they had brutally attacked Poland. "Yes, I know," was all he said.

On the return journey from the dentist we called in at the café and were warmly welcomed by Helga, the guard's girlfriend. She brought us two mugs of hot steaming coffee. To me this was a great treat, having for years drunk horrible ersatz coffee or herb tea. I noticed a wireless on a shelf above the table. "Can I turn it on?" I said. "Yes, but not too loud," said Hans (we were now on friendly, first name terms). I fiddled with the dial and suddenly we were on B.B.C World Service. I had my ear close to the wireless set writing the latest war news down on a serviette.

Hans was looking romantically into Helga's blue eyes when suddenly the café door opened, then closed with a louder bang, causing the three of us to look round sharply. Just sitting down at a table was a S.S. officer, a Major, with a black patch covering one eye. His chest had rows of campaign medals and clasps. Hans jumped up like a rocket, exclaiming, "Komm, komm, schnell, schnell," and we made for the door to make a quick exit. It was well known that anyone listening to the B.B.C. world news was committing a capital offence, punishable by death. My heart missed a few beats as Hans pushed me forward. As we passed the S.S. officer, he looked up at me with a long hard gaze. I expected hard loud words of command – but there was just a hardening of his lips, together with a slight movement of the head pointing towards the door. I mumbled to him, "Danke schön, Herr Major," and was outside into the fresh air.

Hans was trembling and in something of a state of shock, and I must admit I was confused. I said to him, "How did we get away with that"? But Hans was speechless. The few S.S. men I had met in the past had been cold, ruthless killers, but here in the café we had met one that was human.

Talking to Hans later, we both came to the conclusion that the Major was a professional soldier who had seen a lot of the horrors of war and who knew that if he reported us, he would literally be passing the death sentence on two men, one of his own countrymen and one of the enemy. I would have liked to have contacted that Major after the war to thank him and ask him what exactly passed through his mind in those few seconds in a village café. As we were walking up the track to the camp, Hans kept muttering, "We could have been slaughtered." Once again, the fortunes of war. I believe that one of the determining factors which influenced the S.S. officer was that he was a mature man in his forties, and so was not easily swayed by Goebbels' propaganda.

In 1944 when the fighting in Italy was becoming a 'slogging' match, with heavy casualties being suffered on both sides, captured Allied wounded were being evacuated to the rear of the fighting line and put on hospital trains to be transferred to P.O.W. camps in southern Austria. On one occasion, a hospital train arrived at the local station and the wounded were brought into our camp. We had no medical room. People were moved around, turning one hut into a medical ward. There were about a dozen wounded men in single bunks, who were being looked after by a Medical Officer who had been captured with them. He was a very competent doctor and popular with the men.

Having got the wounded men settled down, he came to me and said, "I want you to help me with this particular wounded man." He was an American G.I. with his face completely covered in bandages. "I'll explain tomorrow," said the M.O. With that he slumped on a bunk and was immediately fast asleep.

The next morning the doctor came to me and said, "I want you to sit by this G.I. until he comes round. He has received severe face wounds and when we stopped off at a hospital in Tarvisio he had an operation on both eyes. Unfortunately he will never recover his sight, so comfort him as much as you can." As I sat by the side of the American, he became conscious and began to talk. I encouraged him to talk about himself as I thought it would be somewhat therapeutic for him. Eventually his story came out. He was 18 years old and came from a community in North Dakota. All the inhabitants had originated from Germany before the war. The nearest town to their community was eighty miles away. The first time he had tasted tea was when he was handed a mug of it on arriving in Scotland when he landed from a troopship. He said that he spat out the tea immediately. At home he drank only milk. He was an infantryman whose unit had landed in Italy near Anzio and had gone into action immediately. In the battle, the Germans counter-attacked fiercely and all he remembered was a blinding flash and no more.

The following day he suddenly said to me, "Can my sight be cured?" I said, "You will receive the best medical attention, don't worry." Our conversations went on for several days, but I could see that the horrible truth that he may be permanently blind was beginning to dawn on him. One morning I went in and sat beside his bunk. He took hold of my hand and quietly said, "I want to ask you something. I want you to swear on God's honour. Am I going to be permanently blind?" A dilemma now confronted me. I gripped his hand tightly (one of the most comforting gestures when one wants reassurance) and gently said, "The Medical Officer said there is no opportunity here for further medical treatment. You will have to wait until you can be taken to a hospital where there are the latest treatments available for the eyes." This seemed to put his mind at rest. He gave me a tight squeeze of the hand and said, "Gee, thanks pal." I thought he should be given more time to ponder a lifetime of living in a dark tunnel, and at least a period of time in this condition to soften the blow.

The next day he seemed more relaxed. My words had evidently cheered him up. I turned into my bunk that night with mixed emotions. I continued to sit with him daily for about a week. Suddenly, during one night whilst I was asleep, he was evacuated. I didn't even have the chance to say goodbye to him, but that was nothing unusual in the Army.

One morning, just after dawn, heavy explosions could be heard coming from the north from the direction of Munich. It was at a time when anything that moved in daylight was a fair target for Allied aircraft. I remember at a later date, when American Thunderbolt fighter bombers, flying at almost ground level, attacked a heavily-marked Red Cross train on the railway line that ran close to our camp near Spittal in southern Austria. How could Allied pilots fail to see the clearly-marked red crosses on the carriages?

Fig: 23. The P47 'Thunderbolt, was used in large numbers by the USAAF for ground attack duties. By late 1944, they ranged far and wide over German-held territory, attacking trains, vehicle convoys and virtually anything else that moved!

On another occasion towards the end of the war, a seriously wounded casualty needed a leg amputation. Because of the constant Allied day and night bombing, medical supplies were running short. The Medical Officer said to me, "All I can administer in this case is strong local anaesthetics. I have explained this to the patient who, in my opinion, is a very strong character." The operation was to be performed on a trestle table. At least it was daylight or there would have been even greater problems.

I was to act as theatre orderly for the operation. As we were preparing the room and collecting the necessary equipment, the Medical Officer said in a hushed voice, "I shall have to do some bone sawing, can you go and see the German Adjutant and ask him if he has a gramophone and some suitable records. You will be required to play some music when I start the sawing. The noise of sawing upsets the patients more than anything. All you have to do is play the record when I nod."

I recalled having seen an old fashioned gramophone complete with horn in the Adjutant's office. I saw the Officer and explained to him the Medical Officer's request. He went to the pile of records and chose one, saying, "This is the best record for the occasion." He handed to me Richard Wagner's – 'The Ride of the Valkyries'.

I sat in a corner of the room as the operation was about to commence. The Medical Officer gave me a nod. I placed the record on the turntable, wound up the machine and out of the horn came the rolling cadences of Wagner, somewhat distorted, but the decibels were entirely appropriate as we followed the old Norsemen charging across the heavens. Reaching the end of the record, and with another nod from the M.O., I furiously wound up the machine and the Norsemen's charge started again. The operation was then over. The patient was remarkably self-possessed. I thought to myself that one day I'd be able to say, "I've seen it all, even playing my part in a surgical operation."

During a monthly visit from the M.O., he treated me for a painful varicose vein in my leg. He said, "Take your trousers off and stand on that trestle table." I did as ordered and, quick as a flash, he plunged a needle into my leg. Whether he was tired or whether the needle was blunt I know not, but a spurt of blood went shooting across the room. "Sorry, old chap," he said, "Better luck next time." I knew then that in future, I would have no fear of surgery.

I had witnessed many incredible incidents in a relatively short space of time, but the most extraordinary one of them all was the sight of an American airman falling out of his aircraft from several thousand feet up – and surviving.

During the winter of 1944/45, each day when the visibility was clear, we would watch large numbers of American Flying Fortress and Liberator bombers from bases in Italy winging their way to bomb Munich and southern Germany. They were escorted by Lightning and Mustang fighters, which constantly weaved around the bombers' flanks. Should the fighters see any suitable targets down below, they would peel off and attack them. Against the blue winter skies they made a brave sight, leaving long vapour trails stretching for miles behind them. With the war moving towards its end, the Luftwaffe was nowhere to be seen. After midday we would look up into the skies, our eyes following the planes returning to Italy. They flew in groups of about ninety planes in each group. We would try and count whether any planes had been lost over their target.

On one raid, the bombers had been attacked by German fighters over their target and their formations had been broken up. The bombers were now wending their way back to base individually. We could hear the sputtering of a plane's engines. One lone Flying Fortress, obviously in great difficulty, could be seen clearly against the snowy background of the Gross Glockner mountain range. It was losing height, and dark smoke was pouring out of its engines. We then saw the crew baling out, one by one. Parachutes fluttered open – all but one – and we saw a black dot falling all the way down to the snow. He was a crew-member whose parachute had failed to open.

Fig. 24. The Boeing B17 'Flying Fortress'. The principal heavy bomber used by the USAAF in Europe during WWII. Two of these aircraft, at different times and as a result of enemy action, crashed in the vicinity of the camp where the author was held during 1944 and early 1945.

The Commandant of the camp had also seen it. He phoned through to the Barracks in the village, where a detachment of Alpine ski troops were stationed. They went in search of any survivors from the crashed plane. Returning to their camp with the crew, they reported that some of the detachment had remained to search for the missing airman. Later that day we were told the searchers had located him and, instead of finding a dead body, they had come across the pilot alive in deep snow, with apparently nothing seriously wrong with him apart from a broken leg and a mass of bruises. He had fallen at an angle into the snow, which had broken his fall. He had been put on a mountain rescue sledge and taken down to the village, then on to a local hospital where he was attended to by a couple of nurses, who were more interested in trying out their English on him, than in his injuries.

A few days later he hobbled through the gates of our camp to resounding cheers. He told us that the Fortress had been in difficulties and flying very low when he baled out. After pulling the ripcord of his parachute, he suddenly realised nothing was happening and then he plummeted into the snow and blacked out. Regaining consciousness he looked up and saw the track he had made sliding down the snow-covered slope. He was certain that the heavy flying gear he was wearing, together with the deep snow he had fallen into, had contributed to his survival. His rescuers had strapped him on to a mountain sledge and insisted he drink a hefty swig of schnapps, so that he would be totally oblivious to the speed and the steepness of the journey down to their base camp. Before leaving our camp to go to an American Flyers' camp, he drew up a document asking the rest of his crew and our Camp Commandant to sign, proving they had witnessed his incredible fall and survival.

Escapes And Working Camp

In the camp there were long periods of extreme boredom, which often showed itself in bizarre behaviour.

One winter's afternoon, when the snow outside was so deep we could not even walk around the compound, we were all lying on our bunks either dozing or reading. Occasionally a man would get up and wander around a bit, stretch and then return to his bunk. On one occasion a glider pilot called Philip, a naturally morose character, and a Polish American, called Johnny Bernatzick, got down from their bunks at the same moment and moved towards the same stool. Each of them claimed possession of the stool and they stood glaring at each other. There followed an exchange along the lines of; "That stool is mine." "No it isn't, it's mine." "Let go or I'll punch your bloody nose". "You just try it." At that, the stool fell to the floor and they started going at each other hammer and tongs, only stopping when both were exhausted.

A voice from the sidelines said quietly that they ought to wait for Spring, then finish it off outside. The two men absorbed this advice, shook hands and went off happily together to clean themselves up.

Both captors and captives suffered from frustrations as the war ground on.

One day we were all outside, enjoying a stroll in the warm sunshine, when a shot rang out and, automatically, we all dropped to the ground. We looked up to see one of the guards still pointing his gun into the compound. We later learned that he was from Cologne and that he had just been told that his wife and children had all been killed in an air raid. When questioned, he told the Commandant that he was just evening up the score a little. A few days later he was posted to the Eastern front.

For the Germans, the war news was becoming grimmer by the hour. They were suffering heavy reverses on the Russian front. We ourselves knew clearly that the Russians would eventually bleed the German army to death. As we talked to the guards we could understand their feelings and concerns. Many of them who had served on the Russian front were now worried about the outcome. We on the other hand, were feeling more optimistic and confident about the future.

Fig: 25. Our camp orchestra, Spital, 1944.

Conditions in the Camp had improved. For once the war seemed remote. We were receiving Red Cross parcels regularly. Not even one Allied bomb had been dropped locally. A concert party had been arranged and a stage built. A batch of musical instruments had been received from the Swiss Red Cross. I was once again able to play a violin. We wrote sketches and produced musical plays. These were being performed to packed houses. As there were no seats, everyone sat cross-legged on the floor. A great deal of skill was being attained in the making of stage costumes from pieces of material we had scrounged.

Our female impersonator, who went by the nickname of 'Fanny', was a roaring success and by far the most popular entertainer in the party. He flounced around the stage, and was quite indistinguishable from the real thing. This went on for a while until some of the men began poking fun at Fanny by passing remarks that he was a homosexual. We had experienced trouble with homosexuality at a previous camp and it became a touchy subject. Fanny had struck up a relationship with the leading man in the shows, 'Big George' as he was fondly called. I felt sure this was a natural friendship but Fanny and George began to feel the strain of the leg-pulling, so they both decided to have a go at opting out of the camp.

This led to the most amusing attempt to escape from Stalag 18a. It was by now 1944. The present Commandant possessed a sense of humour, unlike his predecessor who had been a Prussian, and had acted like one. An Escape Committee was formed to give the 'escapees' every assistance possible, however they didn't appear to need much. One day Fanny and George just walked out of the camp. The best escapers always studied carefully the movements of every person in the camp. With Fanny and George it was extraordinarily simple. A working party of local peasants, who were unfit for military service, and a number of Russian slave workers were engaged in the re-building of part of our wash house, which had been falling apart. They came into the compound every morning and returned home or to their barracks in the late afternoon. One of the guards had poor eyesight, so the escape was to be made on the day he was on duty.

Fig: 26. The camp gymnasium at Spital, 1944.

The working party was under the foremanship of a local man named Toni, with whom we had formed a friendship by giving him English cigarettes from our Red Cross parcels. The Escape Committee, having made an arrangement with Toni, supplied him with an additional quantity of cigarettes. He passed out through the gates with his squad of workers, happy at having his pockets full of cigarettes. An additional bribe was three blocks of Cadbury's chocolate. On the day of the escape, two additional characters tagged on to the rear of the working party as it made its way out of the camp. We all held our breath as Toni chatted to the short-sighted guard. We then watched as Fanny, dressed as a female peasant, and George as an Austrian peasant with a typical Austrian hat on his head, all made by our Props' Committee, walked out into the nearby pinewoods and disappeared. We celebrated by shaking hands and patting each other on the back.

A few days later we were amazed to see Fanny and George returning back through the same gates they left by, with a very amusing tale to tell. Having gone into the woods they had moved as quickly as they could in case the alarm was raised. They found a cosy barn above the valley and slept the night. The following day they moved south to the Yugoslavian border. In the afternoon, as they approached a farmhouse, they heard the clucking of hens in an outhouse. George told Fanny to stay behind a wall, which seemed quite safe and went on an egg-gathering expedition. Fanny dozed off, with his back against a hedge, still dressed in the peasant girl's outfit. Suddenly awakened by a German male voice, Fanny opened his eyes to see a German Oberleutnant standing over him. He asked him/her what she was doing. Fanny said in his halting German that he was a foreign worker, working at a farm down the valley and had been given time off as he had just recovered from an illness.

The Officer, on leave from the Russian front and smelling strongly of schnapps, said he was the son of the farmer whose eggs George had gone to steal, sat down beside Fanny and began to get amorous. Fanny was fighting a losing battle, but kept up the charade until the last moment. The German's amorous advances were getting too much for Fanny. He tried to get up and run but was not strong enough. A swift reach of the German's hand up Fanny's skirt and all was revealed. In the meantime, George had returned with an armful of eggs. On hearing voices he watched the comedy of errors taking place through a gap in the hedge. When the Officer had recovered from his astonishment, George heard him tell Fanny he had been told while in the village that two British prisoners of war had escaped from their camp. When he asked Fanny where his friend was, George decided the game was up and came out from his hiding place.

The Officer burst out laughing and George and Fanny, realising they had been unlucky in having been caught, appreciated they had been caught by a German Officer with a sense of humour. The Officer said, "This is my parents' farm, so you will now join me for a meal before I hand you over to the police in the village." As they went into the farmhouse they were welcomed by the Officer's parents, given a huge meal of herb omelette, followed by schnitzel and large glasses of local wine. The Officer said, "When I get back to that accursed Russian front, I shall have a tale to tell my comrades which they will never believe." When he handed them over to the police, he gallantly said to George and Fanny, "Better luck next time." George could not resist saying to him, "We hope that, should you be in the same position as we have been, you have the good fortune to meet the same sort of person as we have." A shake of the hands and, "Auf Wiedersehen," and they parted.

George was one of the most incredible characters I ever met during my time as a P.O.W. His escapades are unforgettable. They also prove that no matter what obstacles are put in the way, there is always one man who can buck the trend – and successfully so.

After having received the exhilarating news of the D-Day landings, we realised there was still much fighting to be done and it seemed likely we would be spending another bitter winter in captivity. One day in September 1944, at a P.O.W. camp in the Austrian province of Karnten, the combined brains of the Escape Committee had been hard at work in several directions but George, by nature a lone wolf, just walked out. We were sitting in the autumn sunshine, stretched out with our backs to the hut, watching a group of young Austrian girls walking by. They were responding to our wolf whistles, by tossing their heads in a seductive way.

George suddenly stood up and said, "That's made my mind up, I'm off." He then calmly said, "Just watch me. I'm going to get out, it's now or never." He then pulled off the most outstanding escape, by simply walking out through the gates. Then, incredibly, he 'escaped' back into camp using the same method. It was done in the most casual way. He had said to me a number of times, "I'm a lone wolf, just watch me." I never knew of George's background apart from him having been an Infantry Staff Sergeant, but he was a most remarkable man.

The war had now reached a stage where the Germans were calling up every man they could lay their hands on, and consequently the quality of the guards at the camp was noticeably lower. One thing in particular was that almost all the replacements possessed weak eyesight. At the same time, the low rumble of artillery fire could be heard all day, causing our morale and our adrenaline levels to leap upwards. The Allied armies were steadily advancing further north and were by then not far from the last natural barrier – the River Po. This, together with a sky full of silvery vapour trails which were getting more numerous every day, heading in the direction of Munich and many other German cities, gave us more and more hope.

George confided in me that he had had a stroke of luck. His German had been steadily improving when he became friendly with an Austrian odd job man who came into the camp to carry out maintenance repairs. After some hard bargaining with him, George had traded an Austrian jacket and a hat with a feather, for a stock of English cigarettes together with several tins of corned beef. Now, all he had to do was get out of camp.

"How are you going to do that?" I said, "Blow a hole in the wire?" "Oh no, do you remember that previous escape when Fanny dressed as a woman and we tagged on to a working party and got out of camp? Well, next week, another working party is coming in." I said to George, "It worked once, I don't think it can happen again." "Well," he said, "nothing ventured, nothing gained." We sat and we waited.

The latest guard on the gate had a really pronounced twitch in his eye, which we regarded as a good sign for George. Going into the hut we saw George wearing the old peasant jacket and battered felt hat with the feather sticking out. We agreed with him that he looked perfect for his escape. A couple of weeks later we watched a typically shabby Austrian workman join the tail end of six others shambling through the gate. They were so tired they never glanced back. The guard never even looked at them. He must also have been tired. The gate clanged behind him and George was gone. He had done it.

That evening at the normal roll call, George was missed. We knew that, after intensive questioning, the Camp Adjutant, Kreiger, would know how the escape had been made. We could see him ranting and raving at the guard, whose prolonged twitching of the eyes could have been a sign that he was about to be transferred to the Russian front.

For the next few weeks our thoughts were on George's escape, how he was faring and should we see him back? Then one morning, as I watched the incoming workmen coming through the gate, I looked at the familiar figure of the last one tagging on. To my astonishment, it was George. He had returned dressed in the same outfit in which he had walked out. He nipped into our hut and I followed him. "I ran out of fags," he calmly said. He told me that he had made friends with a Polish girl working on a farm, who supplied him with food and all the pleasures required for a soldier on active service. "So what now?" I asked him. "Well, if I can scrounge a supply of cigarettes, I'll be off again." "This time," I said, "it's not going to be so simple. Look out of the window." Standing at the main gate, an excited group of people had gathered round the guard who was saying to them, "I definitely let seven men in and not six." It appeared that one of the staff had said he had seen someone similar to George come into the camp.

In the meantime, we had to hide George. Some time previously, we had begun, then abandoned, a tunnel starting from under one of the huts. We had placed the flagstones back over the entrance, so we quickly raised them, put George down there and pulled the wood-burning stove back into place over the access hole in the floor. This meant we would be unable to light the stove for a while. Then the search for George took place. He could not be found, and we taunted the searchers with sarcastic comments as they rummaged here, there and seemingly everywhere. Slowly, they became inclined to believe it had been a genuine mistake on their part. After all, who would dream of a P.O.W. breaking back into camp? It was ludicrous. But George did.

George then set his inventive brain to work on yet another escape plan. Every two weeks a swill cart, drawn by two oxen, came into the compound to collect swill from the cookhouse. Driving it was an old Polish character named Josef. George said, "I recognise him as a friend of my Polish girlfriend." In the intervening period, before Josef's next swill collection call, George had made a long tin tube from scrap and acquired a strong sack. His plan was to lie in this sack at the bottom of the cart.

Our own party, whose job it was to load the cart with swill, would carefully do so and position the tube for George to breathe through. Josef was only too willing to cooperate in the escape. If George was discovered, Josef could easily prove he was an innocent party. The ox cart arrived at the main gate on its way out. Josef vigorously prodded his fork into the swill, satisfying the guard. With a sigh of relief we saw the cart disappear down the road. We thought we had now seen the last of George. How wrong we were.

It was mid-January and we had been transferred to a small hard labour camp, tucked away on the edge of a thick pinewood at the bottom of a valley. The camp had only one hut, containing twenty wilful characters. We were to be engaged in constructing a road near the camp. For days it had been snowing heavily, for which we were thankful, as we had been able to put our feet up and take it easy. In spite of this, conditions in the camp were grim and, although we had a wood-burning stove in the middle of the hut, we didn't have any interior lighting, making the evenings dark and the atmosphere dull.

One evening, lying under our blankets, we heard a succession of pinecones being thrown at the window. As I opened it cautiously, a pinecone bounced off my head. From the direction of the wire came the familiar voice, "Any fags to spare, you lads." George was back again.

I never found out what happened to George, the expert P.O.W. escapee. If ever you read this George, get in touch with me pal, for old time's sake.

I managed to stave off my frustrations at this stage by spending a lot of time playing my violin, which had arrived from the Swiss Red Cross in Geneva. I did a deal with the Austrian Sergeant Major, who was Viennese and a keen musician and he agreed to take me into the adjacent compound, which was full of Yugoslavs. They were wild men, tall and handsome with great flowing handlebar moustaches, and over the next few weeks I would sit down with genuine gypsies from Montenegro, who played the most fantastic gypsy music from southern Yugoslavia. I would join them in their playing and would reel off 'Black Eyes' first of all, where I would play the standard melody line and they would embellish this with some fantastic harmonics. I only wish now that I had written down some of those variations. Then would follow Monti's Czardas and then 'Bublitshka', the popular Russian peasant tune. In due course, I met a Russian who was in a working party. He was a guitarist who said he had played in a Moscow café. He had been captured in the fighting in the Pripet Marshes. I was captivated when he played haunting melodies, all in the minor key. I came to realise why these traditional Russian melodies were all in the minor key – they reflected the tragic experiences of the Russian peasantry. After all these years, I am still emotionally moved on hearing melodies such as 'Bublitshka' and my mind drifts back to those years. I wonder whether those musicians survived the war?

Russian P.O.W.s were treated like dogs by the Germans. Their footwear was simply pieces of leather held together with rolls of rag. We always made certain that whenever we were near them we had emptied our pockets of any food, as they were so poorly fed they would steal anything edible we had with us. One Russian, a Sergeant whom I was able to converse with in halting German, came from Gorkiy in the Urals. Although it was a city of a million people, there were very few metalled roads and life seemed to be very primitive there. He told me that he was a telephone engineer and that his ambition in life was to own a wristwatch! It was an indication of the wide gulf in living standards between us and the Russians.

I frequently conversed with Fritz, our new camp interpreter, who came from Alsace-Lorraine. As you may remember, the territory of Alsace-Lorraine had been disputed between France and Germany whenever the map of Europe had been re-drawn and the inhabitants had sometimes been French and sometimes German. It had been French from 1919, until being annexed by Hitler in 1940. Fritz was trilingual and, being unemployed in 1940, he had joined the German Army, as at that time he had thought that his future lay in the New Order, as the Nazis called the new political map of Europe.

He spoke excellent English and because of his political background he was a realist and often used the German term for this – 'realpolitik'. He felt that the odds were now heavily against a German victory and, of course, I agreed with him. Our conversations continued until I had established a confidence and rapport with him.

On one occasion he said to me, "I am very interested in improving my colloquial English. Tell me why, when I listen to you English soldiers, I hear them saying 'something is f...ing good', and then they say 'something is f...ing awful', so what does this word f...ing mean?" I explained to him the meaning of the word and said that in soldiers' parlance it means everything and it also means nothing. But it was definitely not to be used in polite company. He walked away deep in thought, more confused than ever.

He had spent some time in Wien Neustadt. Speaking to me in confidence he said he had friends who had become disillusioned with Nazi propaganda. (I knew from my reading of European social history that this area of Vienna had for many years been a hot-bed of radicals). This was dangerous talk by a German to a British P.O.W. A number of his comrades had been sent to a Penal Battalion on the Russian front, for expressing even mildly antipathetic comments on Nazi ideology.

During one of our conversations he said to me, "Would you like a change from here to enjoy a different life?" He pointed out that in our camp of W.O.s and senior N.C.O.s we did not have to work. However, as the war appeared to be drawing to a close, a working party had been requested to clear forest timber and construct a road in the mountains above the camp. I passed this information on to Sergeant Major Cotman who became interested. He said he would take charge of the project.

It was now August 1944 and the Allies, including a large well-equipped American force, were sweeping through Europe. The Russians had won the decisive battle of Kursk, decimating the German Panzer Armies. Most Germans now realised there was no hope of victory for them and, as a result of Allied bombing, Germany was becoming a vast heap of rubble. When it was all over there would be utter confusion everywhere, but in the meantime they thought we would be more use out of the camp working for them, than in it doing nothing.

Sergeant Major Cotman turned out to be the ideal choice to be leading the working party. Cotman had been a regular Officer in the Indian Army; he had been cashiered, but no one knew the reason why. He had then emigrated to Australia, joined the Australian army as a Private and risen to the rank of Sergeant Major. When he was captured, he was leading an Australian Infantry Battalion. To reach the rank he had in the Australian Army proved he was a tough character, especially having to live down his unmistakable English accent. Cotman did all our organising, while I, who before the war had been trained as a Pitman's Shorthand Writer in preparation for my ambition of becoming a journalist, was chosen to monitor the radio we had 'acquired' and quickly take down the incoming messages before the Germans could zero in on the signal.

Another of our comrades was Petty Officer 'Jumper' Collins who, when his submarine had unfortunately surfaced in the Bay of Naples alongside an Italian Destroyer, had found himself and the whole of the crew captured without a single shot having been fired. We also had amongst us several R.A.O.C. Armourers and a number of battle-hardened Infantrymen who had been involved in the bitter fighting in the desert. Two R.A.M.C. Sergeants and two Royal Corps of Signals Sergeants, together with several New Zealanders and a Maori, made up what appeared to be a truly International Brigade! All of us had been brought together without having been given the details of what was planned. There were 24 of us in all.

In the meantime, life was proceeding steadily at the camp. An occasional Hospital Train would arrive from the fighting in Italy and we would glean details from the wounded of the war's progress, plus information on what they had seen on their journey to the camp. We were therefore able to amass a considerable amount of useful information.

The day arrived when Oberleutenant Krieger told us we were moving to the Upper Camp. He knew nothing of the ulterior motives of his superiors – he was simply following orders. He informed us that the work we were about to do would be good for our health. This prompted the ribald response from the back of the hut, "Balls." With a pained facial expression Kreiger commented, "I can never understand you English." When the word went round that our names had been given to Kreiger as volunteers, from then on we found ourselves ignored by our fellow inmates. It was particularly hard on Cotman, who had always been highly respected. "He must be going round the bend," was the comment. "Bloody hell," said Cotman, "The next few days will be tough, you ought to see the faces of some of these cobbers of mine."

To derisive chants from those left behind, we boarded an antique-looking lorry and were driven to the village of Radenthein, the H.Q. of the Magnacite Factory for whom we would be working at another site. We were the subjects of great curiosity from the local slave workers, as we passed through the village. The lorry then chugged laboriously upwards via a steep lane and through dense black pinewoods, eventually reaching a small hut in a clearing surrounded by the usual barbed wire.

Fig: 27. A group of Dutch prisoners photographed inside Spital camp during 1944. The photograph has an address in Breda, Holland, on the back. Note the branches from pine trees on the hut roof as camouflage.

A Sergeant Oblenski was put in charge of us. His Slav-featured face fitted his name, for we were in what had once been the old Austro-Hungarian Empire. To guard us was a Corporal Wolff Schmidt, a red-faced youth sporting pebble glasses who quickly became nicknamed 'Bog Eyes'. The two other guards, one with a black eye patch and the other walking with a pronounced limp, would have been of little use in chasing any escapees. Our sympathies were with them.

The first morning, after a breakfast of dry bread, jam and a bowl of potato soup, we walked up the track to our starting point. The trees to be cut down had already been marked. We were to work alongside Toni, the local woodsman. A squat, five feet tall figure, wearing a traditional Tyrolean felt hat surmounted by a feather, Toni never said, "Ja, Ja," it was always, "Jo, Jo."

We were split into three working parties, each of four men, with the remainder responsible for road-digging lower down. There was to be a midday meal break of half an hour, when we received another bowl of potato soup, then we continued to work until 5.00 p.m. Another simple frugal meal would be taken when we had returned to the hut almost exhausted. As a result of this hard physical work, we were becoming harder and tougher. In our last camp we had always tried to maintain a high degree of discipline, here we became more casual. Sergeant Major Cotman was answering to his Christian name of Arthur.

One day Bog Eyes, who was now being familiarly called Wolff, came into the compound and began talking to us. He went up to Arthur saying to him, "I have a message for you and for you alone." This was now the procedure; there would be contact with only one person. We were receiving information from the troops wounded in the Italian campaign, who were being off-loaded from the hospital trains at our camp. They had told us about a skirmish having taken place at Udine, just over the border in Italy, when Partisans had attacked German S.S. troops. This information was contained in the note passed by Wolff to Arthur, also telling him to burn the note after having read it.

Our informant had been unable to ascertain the number of casualties. There was news that a detachment from the nearby Slovenian SS Division had passed by the camp at Spittal, bound for the border, obviously to take reprisals. All this information we had passed in the note for Arthur to pass on to Wolff. We were happy knowing this had been a worthwhile first effort on our part.

Sitting in the shade of a conifer tree the next day, Arthur observed, "It's obvious that we have been chosen as the right 'griff' (*slang for information*) gatherers in this area, so by Christ we are going to work in top gear. The Camp Leader in Spittal has been taken into my confidence and in future we should be having a steady stream of valuable information."

Our working day began when we moved off to the allocated area for felling the marked trees. The trees stood about 30 metres high. After spending the last 2¼ years cooped up in various camps with only a few yards of bare beaten ground around us, and having been packed together like sardines in a tin, the scent of newly cut timber was heavenly. I was now learning the trade of lumberjacking, as well as being among a host of interesting characters. All my peacetime life I had enjoyed the ambience of mountain life and now, looking through a gap in the trees, I could see a panorama of mountains everywhere.

The four members of my team were Ian Gordon, a lumberjack from South Island, New Zealand; John Taraki, a Maori also from South Island, New Zealand; 'Jumper' Collins and myself. We worked in pairs and my partner was John. I had great difficulty in keeping up with him. He was over six feet tall with a typical Maori flat nose, and a grin which spread from ear to ear. John was the happiest man I had ever met. He would say, "Come on Albert, it's our turn." We would walk to the tree trunk, taking over from the pair who had finished their stint. While we were waiting we had been making wooden chocks to hammer into the opened gap, as we could not use the cross-cut saw until the gap had been made wider. When almost through, Ian and Jumper would pick up their axes and, standing either side of the trunk, chop away. As the brushwood had previously been cleared, Ian and Jumper had to make a quick exit. When high trees begin to fall they tend to jump sideways, becoming extremely dangerous. With a series of cuts on the downhill side of the tree, we could feel it begin to shiver. A shout of "Timber" from Ian and we scrambled quickly away. There would be a tremendous crashing and splintering of branches as it settled down, and the rising pine dust brought on spasms of coughing.

The final task was to use the cross saw and cut the tree into two-metre lengths, then we dug sapines (long poles with a steel hooked head) into each end of the sawn logs, dragged them slowly forwards and whipped the sapine out with a twist of the wrist. The timber would then career down the mountainside, and at the bottom a two-man ox-wagon team would be waiting to drag them away.

One unfortunate day there was a fatal accident. Another group working nearby had a member originating from Manchester. For some reason known only to him, instead of moving away quickly when the warning shout of "Timber" was made, he ran straight into its path, and was buried underneath the weight of the wood. We immediately began furiously to chop the branches away to free him. When we did eventually reach him he was dead. He was given a military funeral and buried in the village cemetery. I wrote to his parents in Manchester who, after the war, wrote to me saying they had made a visit to Austria to view their son's grave. They enclosed with their letter a sketch of the church.

The weeks slipped by into late September, and our spirits began to dip. Over the years of our captivity we had become fatalistic and could usually resist the up and down roller coaster of emotions engendered by the nature of the latest news. For us the war was not moving to its end fast enough. On our part, we had improved our observations of German military activity, after being supplied with illustrations of their shoulder flashes, which told us which units were on the move.

One hopeful sign was the daily sight of huge streams of American bombers winging their way towards Munich and southern Germany. One day we saw a swarm of Mustang fighters attacking a target in the next village. Large clouds of black smoke were rising skyward. We were elated. This elation became somewhat dampened when a detachment of S.S. troops arrived at the camp. Having already been at the receiving end of their brutality, we knew what to expect. They jumped out of their trucks and immediately opened fire over our heads with their sub-machine guns, roaring, "Ausgehen, Ausgehen," (G*et out, get out!*). German orders are always in duplicate and as loud as possible. We understood quite clearly and moved fast, knowing they would have no compunction about wasting their breath shouting out another command. To them, bullets spoke louder than words.

We were marched to the next valley. An area of woods near to the lake of Millstatersee and a number of vehicles were ablaze following the air attack. We were issued with flails to try and stamp out the fires. When an S.S. Sergeant felt we were slacking he fired a short burst over our heads. Should he have killed one of us, he would have been quite indifferent, as our lives meant nothing to him. We knew the S.S. were equally ruthless against innocent and defenceless civilians and Prisoners of War. We also understood the terror that entered people's hearts at the mere sight or mention of them.

Having put the fires out, we were sitting by the roadside waiting to march back to the camp when an S.S. Private strolled by, stopping to stare at us. He seemed to want to speak to us. One of our number asked him in German, "You look weary, have you travelled far in the last few days?" He replied, "Yes, all the way from those accursed mountains the other side of Lubliana." "It must have been tough with all those partisans around." "It was. We were attacked four times on our way here. We have lost about 25 men. But we got level with them one day at Jesenice Gorensko – we shot ten of them in an ambush and then shot fifty civilians to teach them a lesson." "What a thing to do to poor old civilians." "Well there's a war on isn't there, so what's the difference between soldiers and civilians?"

Now we were intelligence-gathering wherever we could by using our military experience. We would look carefully at the German's shoulder and sleeve flashes and compare them with the facsimiles with which we had been provided. Through the conversation with this German S.S. Private, we knew the name of his unit, its strength, and an account of the casualties it had suffered on its route through Slovenia. These were then passed back by radio to our intelligence people and were processed. We were 'doing our bit'.

There was one occasion when we all cooperated fully with the Germans.

The allied bombing had increased greatly, heavily disrupting the transport system, which in turn meant that our food supplies had become very irregular. We were told by the Commandant that the potato crop was ready to be lifted, and there was a dire shortage of men to do this arduous work. If we were prepared to forget about the Geneva Convention and help with lifting the potatoes, we could bring back as many as we could carry for our own consumption. Our committee meeting lasted all of ten seconds and we agreed to cooperate.

As we assembled at the camp gate, the Commandant told us that there were SS in the village and so we had better be very careful about smuggling potatoes into the camp. We took the point and went to work with a will. When we marched back into camp, we must have looked like a bunch of Michelin men, with trousers and battle dress blouses stuffed with potatoes. For the next week or so we gorged ourselves on potatoes, until a voice commented, "I'll never be able to look a potato in the eye again!"

There were some slave labourers in the village at that time, among whom were a group of Polish girls and one of them was heavily pregnant. She worked just the same as the others, until one afternoon she moved to a hut with another girl. A short time later they reappeared with a baby. They were sent to the village by the Overseer and we were told that they would be allowed two days off.

One day we took a handcart into the village to collect rations and we saw a group of Russian prisoners loading the body of one of their comrades onto a rough cart. We were told that the local Gauleiter had considered that the man was not working hard enough, so he had pulled out his Luger pistol and shot him in the head. His comrades, after sharing his pitiful possessions among themselves, took his body to a pit outside the village, where it would be covered in quick lime and a handful of earth.

From our camp we could see the area where the pit was, and we kept a tally with notches on the end of a hut. By the end of the war there were 120 notches. When the British Intelligence team reached us, we showed them our evidence and told them what we knew of the Gauleiter's activities. They immediately interviewed him and of course he denied all knowledge. When he was told that he and his staff would personally be digging up the bodies, he admitted everything.

Whenever the Germans spoke of the Russians, they always referred to them as "Unser Menschen" and they treated them with unbelievable cruelty. It was also obvious that most German civilians were aware of this treatment and of that meted out to the Jews. In fairness however, they were all caught up in a situation, where to step out of line in any way brought down on them the same treatment they had seen being imposed on others. Virtually any view which did not fall into line with the Nazi view was punishable with beheading, or at the very least, consignment to a concentration camp.

After the attempt on the life of Hitler in 1944, those found guilty were suspended from meat hooks to die a slow and agonising death. It was all filmed and the population were obliged to attend cinemas and watch these awful events, as a lesson in what happened to dissenters.

Such things should not be forgotten.

One day, Bog Eyes struggled into the hut carrying a heavy box containing our usual rations. He quietly said, "There's a radio receiver in the bottom of the box with instructions on how to use it. Always tune in on the wavelength given initially at 23.50 hours for about two minutes." That evening 'Sparky' Jones reported having fixed a length of wire looped into the ceiling and the radio was in working order. We understood that the intelligence centre was based in Ancona on the Adriatic coast, and from there messages could be beamed to Fitzroy Maclean's Mission somewhere in the mountains of Slovenia. I had no problem taking the information down in shorthand, having had plenty of opportunities to practise it in the past. Within a week, Arthur had compiled a dossier, giving details of German military movements and troop morale. To us these were now halcyon days and we were certainly not vegetating any longer.

Arthur received a warning to get out of the compound at 11.30pm on a specified evening and make his way to a forest clearing. We were also supplied with a golden gift to a P.O.W. – a pair of wire cutters. The party that was to go consisted of Arthur, Johnny the Maori and George the fluent German speaker. The hut door being locked every night, they slipped out through one of the windows, crawled to the wire, made a few quick snips and they were out. Arthur later said he had to admire Johnny's skill at finding the clearing on a pitch-black night. There they met Bog Eyes, together with two Czech foreign workers, one of them referred to as 'The Colonel'.

There was a fair-sized contingent of Czech workers of technical ability in the area. They, like us, believed the war would soon be over, and had secretly formed themselves into a group to be of assistance when the Allies arrived. The Allied forces were sweeping across France and nearing the German borders. A big offensive was taking place in Italy, from where we could hear the faint rumbling of artillery guns. On the Eastern front, the Russians were pushing the Germans back with ease.

On their return to the hut, Arthur reported to us that contact had been made with the Czechs who were, in his opinion, enthusiastic but naïve. Their leader was referred to by his people as 'The Colonel', though no details had been forthcoming of his military experience. Further contact was to be made with the Czechs, but we had to proceed cautiously, as there were inherent dangers if anything leaked out to the Germans.

Our party had agreed to meet the Czechs weekly, but as time went by the pace of the Allied attacks appeared to be slowing down. There was now a haunting fear that we might still be incarcerated in the camp by the time Christmas arrived, and we began to lose our cockiness. We were returning to the old P.O.W. syndrome of having up and down emotions.

One night Arthur awoke in the early hours to see one of the New Zealanders called Harry, who had joined him through the wire earlier on, climbing back through the window into the room. "Where have you been?" Arthur asked him. He said the Dutch girl, who was in the party he had met earlier in the evening, had agreed to meet him later. He had slipped out quietly on his own again and met her. "You bastard," yelled Arthur, waking up the whole hut. "You are putting us all at risk. If the Germans find out about this we shall all be for the chop."

He said to Arthur, "She told me she was anti-Nazi." "Did you say anything else to her?" bellowed Arthur. "No," was the answer, "I was too busy satisfying her." "If I catch you going out to her again, I'll have your guts for garters," said Arthur. Having never regarded this man Harry, who was half-Maori and a loner, as reliable, we dropped off to sleep ill at ease.

Two days later in the morning we were preparing to set off for work, when a friend of Bog Eyes from the village rushed into the camp and into our hut saying, "A unit of the S.S. are making their way up here." Confusion reigned. Panic caught even the camp guards. It was amazing how the very word S.S. struck cold fear into everyone – friend or foe. We smashed the radio and cut up the aerial wire. A stock of Reichsmarks we had been supplied with were pushed into the stove and burned.

All hell was let loose as the S.S. troops charged into the hut, one of them felling Arthur with his rifle butt as he began to protest. The floor and the ceiling were systematically torn apart and searched. We were in big trouble. These S.S. were obviously a bunch of cut-throats. Their Oberleutnant stood erect, his legs apart, in the centre of the hut, and watched his men with a cold fish expression on his face, no doubt disappointed so little had been found apart from a few charred radio parts and burned Reichsmarks. These were laid out on the floor. We were pleased the evidence was so small – at least for the time being.

Short barked words of command from the Officer and we were herded together in tight groups, taken outside and down to Radenthein. We tramped through the village streets, which were devoid of inhabitants. Reaching a building, which appeared to be a Works' Office, we were unceremoniously pushed and kicked inside, and found ourselves in a large bare room. While sitting around, Arthur's advice to us was to remain tight-lipped, pointing out, although feebly, that we were entitled to the support of the Geneva Convention. Arthur then turned to Harry and said, "That so-called friendly Dutch girl was evidently a Nazi sympathiser and an S.S. plant." No comment came from Harry. We were to be in for a long, painful and unpleasant time.

That night we curled up on the cold, hard, wooden floor, huddling together to keep warm, each one of us remaining awake, deep in our own thoughts. In the morning, Arthur was the first one to be called out for interrogation. "Trap one for me," was his comment. Eventually I was dragged out and pushed into another room. I was ordered by an officer, who spoke perfect English, to sit down and answer his questions. Sitting at the table were also two civilians, obviously members of the Gestapo. One of them did most of the questioning, while the other wrote down notes. Standing directly behind me were two hefty S.S. troopers, evidently 'gentle' persuaders. The first statement made to me was, "You have no protection from the Geneva Convention as you have attempted to abrogate the powers of the German Government and seditiously stirred up peaceful workers to connive with British Intelligence. Firstly, to save your skins, you must tell us the name of your German contact." To which I replied, "I don't know what you are talking about." From behind me came two vicious thumps on the head, felling me to the floor. I was then pulled up and, for what seemed an interminable time, the same questions continued to be flung at me. I gave the same answers and was repeatedly felled to the floor and dragged up again. Finally he said, "If you do not tell us the name of the German traitor, you will be shot and just disappear." All I could reply to him was, "If you say we are in contact with British Intelligence, then they will soon know which German individuals are responsible for our deaths, then you yourselves will be shot when the war is over, which won't be long." After a further thumping from the back, I was taken out. I felt happy that I had scored a bull's eye against the S.S.

I was then thrown into another room, joining the others who had been interrogated. There were a few bloody noses but morale was exceptionally high. When the last one was pushed into the room, there was a pause until a Gestapo man walked in. "As you have refused to cooperate with us you will be taken out at dawn tomorrow and shot." To which Arthur retorted, "We are all registered Prisoners of War at Stalag 18a. If that happens you will all be signing your own Death Warrants." Fine dramatic words, but it was worth a try. As a parting shot to the Gestapo man, Arthur said to him, "You are an educated man and speak English. You may know an English poem which runs, 'I thank whatever Gods may be for my unconquerable soul.'" I myself knew that poem written by Henley and I wondered if the German did.

Another night on the hard floor. At dawn we were led out and lined up outside the offices of the Magnacite plant. Standing nearby was a platoon of German soldiers with their rifles at ease. I was certain this was the end, when a muttered comment was passed among us – "It's all bluff, we are lined up with windows behind us. Firing squads always fire against blank walls." I had never noticed this. After a long pause and a consultation between two Gestapo men, we were told to walk slowly past another window, then stop and look inside. When I looked into the room I saw the so-called Czech 'Colonel', who had been beaten up rather badly. As I stood there he saw me and shook his head.

Conferring amongst ourselves, we came to the conclusion that the Germans were going to concentrate on interrogating the few British P.O.W.s who had, over a period of time, been working in collaboration with the Czech 'Colonel'. I had only met him once and so was soon 'weeded out' and returned to the camp. Five remained behind for more intensive questioning. We were told at a later date that they had survived. The remaining nineteen were sent back to the camp. From now onwards we had to live on hard rations of potato soup and dried bread only. All the camp staff were posted away and replaced. We never found out whether they caught up with Bog Eyes.

For two months we worked on building a road through woods, where we were supervised by a renegade Pole. The guards were unfriendly but we were to get our own back on them. We found scattered about numerous flat stones. When the supervisor wasn't looking, we dug deep holes in our section of the road. By not building up the stones in a proper way we placed the flat stones over the holes, covering them with larger stones to hide the flat ones. We would have been delighted to have been there when the first loaded lorries came down the road. If the driver lost control of his wagon he would have finished up at the bottom of the valley. Unfortunately, if and when this happened, we had already moved on.

As the weeks rolled by we recollected our previous existence at Stalag 18a. The weather had now turned colder and light falls of snow crept in from the surrounding mountains. We found stone breaking becoming harder. As a result, we were given larger portions of potato soup. After finishing work and arriving back at our hut in the late afternoon, we brought tree branches we had collected to put in the wood-burning stove. Then we stood around swinging our arms and stamping our feet to get the blood circulation moving. A tin mug of tea was like nectar, followed by a dixie of potato soup. This was a great improvement on the bread and water on which we had previously existed. One of our number, 'Geordie,' of the Northumberland Fusiliers, and a staunch Methodist – also a supreme optimist – kept muttering, "Let's be thankful for small mercies," upon which he would be promised a sudden death by one or more of us, and he would soon shut up.

As the snow became deeper, it became impossible to carry on with our road building. We could now hear bursts of gunfire coming from the direction of Yugoslavia and news was filtering through that the village people on the other side of the valley near the Yugoslav border were happy that they were now being protected by Austrian soldiers.

During our captivity in Austria, the days were confined to hard laborious work. Now in winter, with the short days and long dark cold nights, a sense of boredom prevailed. We could only sit around the wood-burning stove – and talk. We spoke of our pre-war days, of our families, of wives and sweethearts. We recalled the horrors we had seen, the traumas we had experienced and the friends we had lost. We spoke of when we would be released, which we prayed would not be long now. We spoke of what the future may hold. We swapped humorous anecdotes from our recent past. There may not have been too many, but there had been some that had kept our spirits up.

Fig: 28. A series of photographs taken at our last camp. Right to the end there was the ever present 'wire'.

The Beginning Of The End!

The winter's snow began to fall constantly, making it impossible for us to work outside. It was also becoming more difficult to collect brushwood for our wood-burning stove. We had to dig ourselves out of the snowdrifts, then struggle to make our way down to the bottom of the valley. It was all very exhausting. We were thankful when we were sent back to Stalag 18a.

On Christmas Day 1944 at Stalag 18a, we were able to enjoy an alcoholic drink – of a kind. It was a brew made from the packets of dried sultanas that everyone received in their Red Cross parcels. There was just enough for one mug for each man. The R.A.M.C. orderly, who was in charge of the camp's medical box, produced a few thimbles of a concoction he said would bolster the alcoholic content of the brew. We had always considered this character partly round the bend, and that opinion was confirmed when we took our first sip of his brew. It had an aroma of rubber solution, but we drank it nevertheless, and how we suffered. We became violently ill, retching all we had drunk into a bucket. He later said he had added a small amount of tetrachloride to the brew! Christmas Day 1944 was a day no one present would ever forget.

In January, February and March 1945, our trek round the wire became a matter of wading through the slush. This was enlivened one day by the appearance of a Cossack Division riding along the road and past the camp. Our Camp Commandant had been warned by his superiors that they would be arriving in the area. He had met them previously when his regiment had been retreating through Yugoslavia. Their lines of communication were being constantly harassed by attacks by partisans, so the Cossack Division had been detailed by the Germans to use any method they thought fit against the partisans. This they did, and when our Commandant passed through several villages as he moved north, he saw long lines of dead villagers by the side of the road, who had been executed by the Cossacks.

The Commandant warned the local inhabitants around the camp to place anything valuable and movable under lock and key. The Cossacks lived off the land and nothing in their path was sacred. We gathered as much information on them and their movements as possible, believing it may be useful when British Intelligence arrived.

One morning, Cossacks struggled in their thousands along the road past the camp. In fact, there were 10,000 of them, including their women followers, as well as carts loaded with baggage. Their commander was a German, General Von Panwitz. His Second in Command, General Krasnov, was a Ukrainian Cossack. Originating from the Ukraine, where many Cossacks lived, they had always been anti-Bolshevik. As the Nazi armies had steam-rollered over southern Russia, these men had volunteered to join and fight for them, wearing German uniforms. They were easily recognisable by their distinctive tall astrakhan headgear.

We were fascinated to see them as they passed along, riding on their small wiry ponies and dragging two long spars of spruce logs, across which were lashed all their possessions. The men had long flowing moustaches, while the women wore long voluminous coats with sheepskin collars and brightly coloured headscarves. It reminded me of pictures I had seen of Genghis Khan, the 13th century Mongol ruler, and his marauding hordes.

In early 1945, the Cossacks who were now passing by our camp, had travelled across Hungary together with the retreating German armies. A German Officer told us that it was the Cossacks who did their dirty work for them. If the advancing Russians were to catch up with them, they would show no mercy and the Cossacks would be executed on the spot. When the British 6th Armoured Division arrived at the end of the war they thought the Cossacks were colourful creatures. (By then they had taken off their divisional identification badges).

After the war, at the Macmillan/Count Tolstoy trial, Tolstoy accused the British of handing the Cossacks over to the Russians who quickly dispatched them. They deserved their fate – they had fought for the Germans wearing German uniforms. Tolstoy was not there to see it. We British P.O.W.s were close to the scene of fighting and shared the same philosophy: 'You are either with us or against us.' Armchair observers are seldom right.

One day an American Flying Fortress bomber came into view with its engines on fire, leaving trailing smoke and losing height. We watched as the crew baled out, their parachutes opening and the men falling down onto the snow-covered slopes. A group of ski troops went out and recovered the crew. When they were brought into our camp, I was able to speak to the pilot, a New Yorker. When we took him for a walk round the camp he commented, "Where are your slit trenches?" I said to him, "What slit trenches? This is a P.O.W. camp with red crosses clearly marked to identify it." To that he replied, "Don't be too confident, buddy. All's fair in love and war." A few weeks later, a stick of bombs landed on nearby Stalag 18a P.O.W. Camp.

The noise of gunfire as the Allies advanced across the Lombardy plain was becoming ever closer. A Company of Hungarian Infantry had encamped near to us, having been brought in to defend the nearby Tarvis Pass. They stared curiously at us, as we were probably the first British troops they had seen. Having decided the war was almost over, they believed it would be politic to be friendly with us. As our Austrian guards had now become more relaxed, we thought we should take advantage of this. 'Jumper' had established a rapport with the Hungarians so we hatched a plot. He was told they had a Medical Officer who spoke good English. Pointing to me, Jumper said that I was suffering from a stomach complaint and could I go and see the Medical Officer. Within a few hours it was arranged.

Jumper and I were let out of the gate with a guard, accompanied by a posse of Hungarians. While trying to impress them by marching in step, I still had to feign having a stomach pain. We arrived at the Medical Officer's tent, coming smartly to attention and saluting him. He said in perfect English, "Stand at ease, gentlemen." He soon realised the 'medical problem' was a ruse to make contact. He dismissed the guard and his troops. Their Commanding Officer, a friendly chap who could not speak a word of English, arrived. They had both seen active service on the Russian front and now realised they had been used as cannon fodder by the Germans. They were now fearful of being taken prisoner by the Russians. Jumper said that Tito was pushing forward up in the mountains of Yugoslavia, supported by a Russian Division.

The Medical Officer said to us, "How can we help you British, for we are your friends?" In the meantime, an Austrian farmer, Joseph Napakoj, who owned the land the Hungarians were camped on, had arrived. A three-way conversation began in German with Jumper. The Hungarian C.O. implied that his men knew the English were honourable people. We suggested that, on behalf of the British, we would draw up a free pardon for the C.O. and M.O. for cooperating with the British P.O.W.s. On a sheet of paper bearing a Hungarian military heading, we wrote out a statement saying they had fully cooperated with us.

The C.O. said their Liaison Officer had been informed by the Germans that an Artillery Unit would shortly be arriving to defend the bridge over the River Gail, which they believed would be the obvious point of entry for the British Army. Before the Hungarians left we could see a number of 40mm guns being off-loaded at the bridge. We hurriedly left, after an assurance by the C.O. that he would be posting some of his troops to support the Germans, but would of course be supporting us. Truly Machiavellian! As we were escorted back to our camp, Jumper was engaged in an animated conversation with our Austrian guard, who told him he would be deserting to make his way home, which was only a few miles away. That night when we turned into our bunks we were all too excited to sleep.

From now on I considered it safe to write a diary, and here it is:

29th April 1945

An exciting day full of rumours – Hitler is dead – Peace terms possible – British 8th Army is near Udine. It is raining heavily and the air raid sirens for once are silent. We are concerned that we are too close to the vital bridge, which is ready to be blown up. I wonder what tomorrow will bring? The main camp at Stalag 18a is on the move to Pongau, 100kms away. In pouring rain, and with little food and shelter, I pity our friends out there and we count ourselves lucky.

Two nights ago the mountains on the Yugoslavian border were lit up by four large fires, which could be seen from here, as the partisans are evidently calling up their comrades for one last push. Our guards are already 'windy', expecting attacks from every quarter. Most of the Reich is already lost, but the square-headed punch-drunk bastards are still fighting. We all wonder what will happen in the next few days. Having been a POW for too long has dulled my emotions. The end has been in sight for so long that I shall not be able to appreciate my release when it actually comes.

On the bombing of this part of Austria: the people of England do not know what air war is compared to the bombing that has taken place here. All this year the air raid sirens have sounded continually. During the daytime, American Flying Fortresses fly over in their hundreds, 'doing over' various targets. In between what we call 'dogies', Thunderbolts, Lightnings and Mustangs attack the railways and any vehicles attempting to run the gauntlet. By night, British Avro Lancaster bombers, on their way to targets, drop candelabra flares and propaganda leaflets. Occasionally, a plane crashes, but not very often. Without a pause there is always the sound of sirens and the drone of aircraft. The local population go below ground. Railway trains only move at night – where the tracks have not been blown up – and the roads are deserted. Sometimes our rations never arrive. There is no certainty about life at all.

A hospital train arrived last night. Among the casualties was a British Officer who had spent three months in an Italian hospital. The whole length of one of his arms was enclosed by a plaster cast. On it was written every possible rude word in both English and Italian.

Tuesday, 1st May 1945

Things are getting more exciting each day. As there is no fear of this diary being confiscated, I can spill the beans on how we are getting the 'griff'. Today I have been over to Furnitz village and listened to the news on the radio in a civilian's house. My shorthand was very shaky as I wrote down about the Red Flag flying over the Reichstag in Berlin, and the invasion of Austria from the north. When I returned to camp and read this out to the lads they cheered like mad.

We are living on our nerves, but the civilians in the village are even more tense than we are. They are looking forward to the arrival of the British troops, but are very apprehensive that the partisans may arrive first and take savage reprisals. It is still raining and low clouds are sweeping just below the surrounding peaks. The partisans must be having a cold time up there, but they'll be as warm as toast when, fuelled by the local Slivovitz, they get hold of the village girls. The road to Villach is thronged with traffic. Lines of civilians are moving in both directions, from Italy into Austria, and from Austria into Italy. Ex-slave workers from the whole of Europe, with rucksacks on their backs, are on the move back to their homelands. All industry and agriculture has collapsed.

Mid-afternoon

Red-hot griff has just come in. The German radio is going to announce the position at 11 p.m. tonight. What does this mean? Is it news of the German capitulation? Phew. The place is simply seething with excitement. The finest moment in my life is fast approaching. I can hardly wait to see those British tanks coming down the road. The Hungarian troops across the road look a miserable lot. They are digging and erecting a road-block of logs ready to lay across the road. We shan't see them for dust when the British 8th Army arrives. In addition to all this, a batch of Canadian Red Cross parcels, sufficient for one parcel per man, has just arrived to joyous cheers from us. We are now rolling in luxury. Surely we shall be out of this place before the bugs arrive again in the summer. Oh, for the feel of my comfortable bed at home, and the thought of my mother's superb cooking sends me almost crazy.

Wednesday, 2nd May 1945
10.00 a.m.

Further red-hot news has just arrived. Hitler is dead and Doenitz has taken over. The Camp Führer has taken off his Nazi party badge. A group of locals standing outside the wire are having a furious 'confab' as to why Austria doesn't pack it in now that all is lost. They are calling Hitler all the names under the sun, having lost everything in this war. They didn't talk like this when we first arrived in Austria a couple of years ago. Thousands of Hitler's photographs on walls and in the houses are being torn down. At a certain village I remember seeing a sign at an entrance saying, 'Juden Verboten' (*Jews forbidden*) which had been placed there before the war. I should think that has already been taken down. Now that the Austrian Government under Carl Renow has been set up, I am sure Austria will throw in the sponge.

3.00 p.m.

At long last, the rain has stopped and the traffic on the road has melted into the trees.

8.00 p.m.

We can't understand it. No aircraft around shooting up all and sundry. The Hungarian M.O. has just been across with the information that the British 8th Army and the British 6th Armoured Division are at Tarvisio, the last Italian town south of the Austrian border, 15km from here.

Friday, 4th May 1945

Had such an eventful day yesterday that I didn't have time to write up this diary. I was on the go from early morning until 11 p.m. Heard several news bulletins on the radio and now the whole camp is wild with speculation. I heard the Gauleiter of Karnten (the political leader of the local area) speak to the people at 8 p.m. and ask them to fight the Bandits. The word bandit is used by the Germans when describing partisans. As we returned to camp, we stopped and talked to the German guard. He told us his unit had been in Udine when the partisans took over, before the British arrived. Bullets were flying around all over the place as they pulled out of the town and came up the pass.

There was a German Engineering Unit camped up in the village under the trees. Yesterday they mined the road bridge, a solid stone structure over the River Gail. As we are close to the bridge there will be plenty of fun if and when it goes up. In the hills will be the safest place to be. Even in the dark we came across long lines of civilians and slave workers walking along the road towards Italy. They look a pitiful sight – men and women with blankets rolled up over their shoulders, carrying packs of all descriptions, trudging along the road. I recalled having seen a similar scene in France when we were moving to Dunkirk, only on that occasion German aircraft were 'straffing' them. Here, military transport was also on the move but we did not see any heavy guns. And most important of all, there was no S.S. around.

Yesterday, before dawn, Jumper Collins and myself 'acquired' a pick-up truck and went down to Villach to collect a supply of Red Cross parcels to issue to the men. What a windfall! To our great surprise we also received a ration of butter. Yes, butter! Something we had not tasted for years. The fruits of victory are becoming obvious. Several of the boys are already being sick.

The Hungarians have now abandoned digging the road traps. I saw three Cossacks on their white horses yesterday, meat for the partisans. The whole area is becoming more and more international.

Heard the B.B.C. news. There is big disappointment, as there is no mention of the 8th Army moving this way. We hope they have only paused temporarily before storming into Austria. Every day now is like a year. The 'dogies' have been over again today as the weather is improving. They did not open fire, but we eyed them cautiously before they flew off. As with millions of Austrians, I look forward to the day when there are no sirens to send shivers down my spine.

8.00 p.m.

Well, the show is over – ALMOST.

At 1 p.m. I heard the news that the German forces in the north had capitulated. The Austrian radio says there will be an Alpine Redoubt.

With the sort of troops we have seen around here, the punch-drunk bastards cannot possibly hold out against the weight of Allied armour much longer.

Monday, 7th May 1945

The civilians and the German soldiers are expecting the partisans to attack from over the Yugoslavian border at any moment. Further east, Unter Drauberg is surrounded by them and under mortar fire. On Saturday the Burgomeister of Gummern was taken prisoner, and the Spittal/Villach train was fired upon. The nearby bridge over the River Gail now had mounted 40mm guns pointing towards the mountains on the Yugoslavian border. American fighters have been sweeping over Villach giving aerobatic displays of strength. All the civilians are asking, "Will the British 8th Army arrive before the partisans?" Otherwise it will be mayhem. Not far away, the local farmers said that through their binoculars they had seen groups of partisans coming from the direction of the border. On their arrival at a farm, they had raped all the females irrespective of age. The farmhouse had been stripped of every single piece of bedding and furniture, loaded on to carts and taken back over the border. Afterwards they set fire to the farmhouse. This grim news created panic across the valley.

Tuesday, 8th May 1945
2.00 a.m.

Retreating S.S. troops are expected to be coming down the road from the pass at any moment. We have contacted the Hungarians and their C.O., who says he has turned colours and decided to become pro-British. He has deployed 300 men in the hills so there may be a battle royal. Remember that we have signed a Free Pardon for him. Absolutely incredible, but true. I'll describe it in more detail later.

2.30 a.m.

Two German S.S. Officers arrived and asked for the Hungarian Officers. We have never talked so fast in our lives, for after all we have some rifles hidden in the roof.

3.45 a.m.

The local police are paying court to us, and we have become the most popular individuals in the valley. They now tell us they are our eternal friends and it has all been the fault of the S.S. They understand the British

Army is expected across the border in a few hours. The S.S. have uprooted their guns and moved off.

9.00 a.m.

I'M FREE!

The greatest moment of my life!

After all the excitement of yesterday, we were up at dawn. Some of the guards who lived locally had already gone home, while the others lounged around showing courtesy to us, and explaining how they had denigrated the Nazis but had been unable to voice their opinions. Joseph Napakog came into the camp with an outsize bottle of his own brewed Slivovitz, a brew of real firewater, but we were careful not to drink too much. We had been told of an escapee from Stalag 18a, who had been befriended by a local girl. She had given him a bottle of her own brewed spirit which had turned out to be wood alcohol. After drinking a large quantity he had been carried back to his camp blind. The M.O. had expressed his inability to do anything for him. This produced a sobering effect on all of us.

It All Draws To An End!

The German troops, having received orders to lay down their arms, were lounging around chain-smoking. Some were euphoric, while others, who came from Northern Germany, wondered what the future held for them. Rumours were spreading about Russian and other European slave workers already taking their revenge.

Eventually, we heard the familiar sound of tanks approaching, from the squeaks of their caterpillar treads and engine revving. Then, the welcome sight of a 'recce' party of British Officers, and eventually scout cars, followed by columns of tanks. As they swept by, the whole camp stood by the side of the road cheering wildly. We all had lumps in our throats and tears in our eyes. A dispatch rider stopped and he was mobbed. We all shook his hand and thumped him on the back. What a scene of great emotion!

A jeep carrying a group of Intelligence Officers came into the camp, and we were ready for them. We had already compiled a list of the 'goodies' and the 'baddies'. Within hours they were typing lists ready to be circulated, and were highly amused to be told about our Free Pardons for the Hungarian Officers. Several hours were spent completing the lists. We were then told we would be flown back to England when sufficient aircraft were available.

One little incident had to be arranged the next day, small but significant. A few months previously, when a group of us were being transferred from another camp and being moved through Fumitz Railway Station, the Station Master came along and confronted one of our party who, by his features, had the appearance of a Jew. The Station Master shouted at him in the usual arrogant Nazi manner, "Juden." Martin Goldman, as he was called, said, "Ja," at which the Station Master grabbed Martin by the collar and kicked him onto the railway line. Martin was a very popular member of our group. As we all surged forward to help Martin up, one of the guards fired a warning shot over our heads. I told this to the Intelligence Officer. He said, "Right, let's go." Jumper and myself were taken to the Station and asked for the Station Master. When he appeared and was confronted with details of the incident, he denied all knowledge. I took him by the collar and kicked him on to the railway track as hard as I could. When he got up, Jumper repeated what I had done. We came back to camp highly delighted.

Three years later, my wife and I were invited to Martin's wedding at Park Lane Hotel. His friends were thrilled to hear the story.

A number of us were anxious to enjoy our new-found freedom as soon as possible. Together with some close friends, with whom we had played music in a small orchestra I had formed at 18a, we approached a small group of Germans lounging around outside the camp, waiting to be rounded up by the British Infantry who were expected shortly. The Officer in charge of them possessed a Citroën car. We told him we required it, and calmly took it. We then announced to the others in the camp that it was our intention to make our way home to England, but in a different way. In addition to myself, were Pat from Nottingham, Albert from County Durham, Bill from Ipswich and William from Mitcham.

I approached an R.E. Officer who had arrived at the camp with our rations. When I told him of our intention to make our own way home via Italy, he said, "Good show. If I were you, I would do the same thing." He handed me an Italian Beretta pistol, some maps of Northern Italy and a fistful of Italian Lira.

The following day we drove out through the now permanently open main gate, making straight for the border, then down the Tarvis Pass to Udine in the direction of Venice. None of us had been abroad into Europe before the war. We were now in a position to see what to us after three years in the bag (P.O.W. camp) was a real luxury – a bed and plenty to eat.

The first night we stayed at an R.A.S.C. camp. We were welcomed and entertained as Royals. Moving on the next day, we headed in the direction of the Mestre causeway leading into Venice. As we were drinking the local vino with some of the residents we had met, a gunfight broke out. It appeared that a number of Tito's men had advanced from Trieste towards Mestre and had been challenged by a squad of New Zealand Infantrymen who were holding the area. Having decided we had already seen enough fighting to last a lifetime and that we had no intention of getting involved in any squabble, we held a council-of-war among ourselves. I decided to make for the Appennines whilst the others decided to go south via the road. Having already met some of the gorgeous Italian maidens, I felt there were sure to be more ahead of us, so now I was a freelance.

As I crossed the River Po I met a number of South Africans who took me round some old German positions near the river, which during the war had been occupied by the Waffen S.S. They had refused to surrender, so the South Africans had brought up a flame-throwing tank and had literally incinerated them. Looking into the dugouts I saw only blackened skeletons with steel clad helmets and parts of leather belts – the metal buckles bearing the words 'Meine Ehre heisst Treue' – 'My Honour is Loyalty'. If ever there was a misnomer, that was it.

The blue hills of the Appennines were ahead, the sun was shining, I had sufficient food and I was moving in the right direction. The first night I stopped at a café in a tiny village where all the residents were eager to try out their English on me. One charming old couple offered me a bed for the night. The next day I passed through the blackened ruins of a village destroyed by fierce fighting. In that area I felt I was being regarded by some of the peasants with suspicion. I understood their feelings; after all, foreigners from many nations had passed their way and had caused wholesale destruction.

On one day of my travels, when I seemed to have walked interminably, the hills were becoming steeper and the villages fewer and farther between. I saw ahead a small peasant's cottage on the edge of a village. By now, I had realised that I was getting the warmest welcome from the poorest villagers, so this cottage seemed to be the most suitable to make a stop for the night.

Nearby, tilling a field, was a girl in her early twenties. As she looked at me suspiciously, I said, "Bongiorno," to which she replied the same. In my halting Italian, I said "Parla Inglese?" (*Do you speak English?*). To which she replied, "No," and came across, but still looked at me with suspicion. I said to her, "Io sono Inglese," to which she replied, "Ah, Inglese, buona." The fact that I had said I was English and she had said "good" was, I thought, a jolly good introduction. I followed this up with "Io sono Prigonierre di Guerra," (*I am a P.O.W.*) which brought from her a flashing smile.

I thought she was a handsome girl. She had full lips, flashing eyes, jet-black hair and a lovely bust. I had been locked away for three long years, and was single and 26 years old. She spoke fast in those musical elongated vowels with which the Italian language is littered. I took her hand and kissed it, and she giggled, saying what I thought was, "Oh, an English Lord." I said, as well as I could in my limited Italian, "Mi scusi Io sono soldati." (*Sorry, I am just a soldier*). I thought so far, so good, and then she asked me to come and meet her father who was working behind the cottage.

She said to her father, "This is an English P.O.W. who has escaped from the Germans." When I told her that I had just walked out of the camp at the end of the war, she said, "Has the war ended?" It had ended a few days before, but here was a family who had not yet heard this – they did not even own a radio. The father was a typical Italian peasant, with a gnarled face and his back bent with heavy work, but he had a pleasant smile. He immediately said, "Come and have a vino." We went into the cottage.

The place was as I had expected – primitive. A dirt floor, a wood-burning stove, a wire strung across the ceiling, from which was draped a thin old blanket dividing the sleeping quarters. There was a rough wooden table and two chairs in the centre of the room. The old chap, who was called Antonio, brought an old wooden box to sit upon. The girl, Maria, bustled around preparing a meal of spaghetti al pomodoro (spaghetti with tomatoes). While it was being cooked, it smelled delicious. Antonio was busy filling my glass. I had to keep restraining him, or craftily pouring it into a crack in the dirt floor when he was not looking, as I was determined not to become inebriated.

Maria placed a large wooden bowl of pasta asciutta in the centre of the table, then filled our bowls. I could not keep up with Maria and Antonio, and excused myself by explaining my stomach had receded after three years of existing on meagre rations. All through the meal Maria had kept topping up her father's glass, although I noticed she was sparing with hers and mine. I could quite clearly see an interesting situation was developing. I had no complaints. As was to be expected, Antonio passed out dead drunk and we both dragged him past the curtain and dropped him on to his bed.

It was a hot evening and had become dark outside. The only light in the room came from a candle sticking out of a bottle. We started to talk and Maria told me her husband had been a soldier. Shortly after their wedding he had embarked for service in North Africa. "Where was he in North Africa?" I said. "In Libya with Graziani," she replied. I said to her, "Do you know exactly where he was over there?" Maria said, "Yes, he was killed in the fighting at Tobruk." I looked at her and said, "That was where I was captured."

Floods of tears came streaming down her face as she clasped my hand across the table. I moved across to console her, placing my arm around her shoulder. We got up and moved through the curtain and on to her bed, oblivious to the father who was in a deep drunken sleep. She said, "I will show you how a simple Italian peasant girl can make love to a cold Englishman." She handed me a bottle of olive oil, asking me to rub it all over her body, then she did the same to me, explaining that although Italy was a strict Catholic country, love will find a way, so a sponge in olive oil worked wonders.

I had intended to spend only one night with them but decided to extend my stay, feeling I was doing more good remaining there. Eventually, after a few nights, I told Maria I would have to go, otherwise the British Army would regard me as a deserter, with dire consequences.

The following morning I left the cottage, said goodbye to Antonio, and set off hand-in-hand with Maria. Walking through the village, all the female residents came to their doors to wave to us, some of them with tears in their eyes. I found the Italians an emotional race. At the end of the village, I gave Maria a long lingering kiss. As I reached and went over the top of the hill, I looked back to see Maria and all her women friends waving. I reflected that my way of going home was preferable to an aircraft seat.

The following day, as I walked down a road used by R.A.S.C. lorries taking supplies to the British Army of Occupation in Austria, I stopped a lorry and told the driver I was an ex-P.O.W., proving it by showing him my P.O.W. dog tag (identity disc). I was given a Field Service Postcard to write to my mother, telling her I was coming back home via a Grand Tour of Italy. I was also given a pound tin of Bruno pipe tobacco, which was a godsend.

The last few days were somewhat ordinary, except for one incident that occurred when I was making my way up a track leading to a mountain village, which looked like a possible place to stay for the night. Suddenly, half-a-dozen scruffy young Italians wearing red kerchiefs around their necks (partisan badges) appeared. They demanded to know who I was. At first I had difficulty in understanding their dialect. One of them broke into German to which I replied in German – my mistake! It now turned ugly, as they appeared to think I was a German deserter. They searched my kit and found the Beretta and, most important of all, a Nazi armband with a black swastika emblazoned on it. This I had taken from the dead body of a German when I searched his pockets for a suitable memento to take home with me. Although I showed them my dog tag, this did not convince them that I was not a German. This was a period after the war when all Europe was on the move, with millions of civilians making their way back home.

They tied my hands behind my back and, as we made our way to the village, I had many kicks aimed at my body. I was by now really scared. All the peasants I had met on my travels through Italy had been very friendly, but what now? I was dragged into the village square, which was already filled with locals, as word of my arrest had gone ahead. Tied to a chair, the noise from the people was intense. Every time I was thumped hard, I went down to the ground, chair and all.

When the noise eventually subsided, an old peasant, sporting a Medici beard, began to interrogate me. He informed me in his poor English that they considered me a roaming German deserter, who had recently been in the area and raped a local girl. When he paused for breath, I kept saying, "I am English." My appearance was not English. My clothing was made up of odds and ends. My looks were not English, I needed a shave and, worst of all, I spoke German. As I pleaded for my life, the audience was enjoying the high drama. I had to think quickly, "Isn't there anyone in this village who has lived in England and can ask me questions to prove that I am an Englishman?"

There followed some excited cross talk and Italian arm-waving among the crowd, before several people, who could barely speak English, stepped forward. A gnarled old man shuffled to the front leaning on a crooked walking stick then, after waiting to get his breath back, said to me, "And where do you live in England?" I said, "In Sheffield." He then told me he had for a number of years worked as a waiter in Bradford. "So you must have been to Sheffield?" I almost shouted at him. "Yes, on many occasions," he replied. "Then ask me anything about Sheffield." I said. He studied me, scratching his almost bald head, as he racked his brains for what seemed an age. The crowd had gone quiet and I waited breathlessly. "Tell me," he said, "how many top class football teams are there in Sheffield and give me their names?" Like quick-fire, I shouted to him and the crowd, "Two, Sheffield United and Sheffield Wednesday, playing at Bramall Lane and Hillsborough, and their colours are red and white and blue and white."

He swung round and, waving his stick at the expectant crowd, shouted, "He can only be an Englishman!" That night, I was treated as a guest of honour in the village. I insisted on sitting in the chair to which I had been bound during my interrogation hours before. A table was laden with the best produce that could be collected from the area and innumerable bottles of vino. The wine was lustily drank, everyone in a state of happy inebriation. I jumped on to the table and shouted, "Mussolini and Graziani, Boooooh – Churchill and Eisenhower, Bravo." A joyous night, never to be forgotten.

For a day or two I continued to enjoy their hospitality. Then the time came once more to move on. As I walked through the tiny castellated arch and out of the village, the villagers had one last surprise for me. They were lined on either side of the street shouting, "Inglese, Bravo." A charming and lovable race the Italians.

One day as I breasted a hill, I looked down and glinting in the ever-present sunshine were the magnificent domes of Florence. This was the end of my long journey. I walked into the Town Major's office, where I was regarded with some trepidation, even though I showed them my now well-fingered identity disc. The Town Major said to me, "You might have taken it off some dead British P.O.W." Admittedly, the enormous movement of misplaced people taking place throughout Europe at the time was causing the authorities serious problems. I told him to send a signal to Spittal in Austria where the Officer who gave me the Beretta was stationed.

I was placed in a room where I had a wonderful view of the Campanile and the Ponte Vecchio. An orderly brought me a tray with a plate of baked beans and a flagon of white wine. For three days I strolled along the banks of the River Amo and marvelled at the fact that a German Officer had refused to carry out Hitler's order to blow up the Ponte Vecchio bridge.

The Last Lap

Two very different events highlight the last lap of my long journey home.

The first was a flight in a USAAF *B25 Mitchell* bomber, from Florence to Naples. This came about as a result of typical American 'can do' attitude.

I had been hanging about in Florence, and the crew of this aircraft offered to fly me to Naples, from where I hoped to get a ship home. Once we were airborne and at our Norman cruising altitude, the crew all sat back and lit up large Havana cigars. They had sat me in the co-pilot's seat and soon I was puffing away just the same as everyone else.

As we cruised along, I commented on the beauty of the multi-coloured patterns of the Tuscan hills far below, intimating that it would be nice to see it all a little more clearly. No sooner had I said this than the pilot smiled and directed me to go down and forward into the bomb aimer's compartment. Once there, it felt as if the rest of the aircraft was behind me, and I had a magnificent view through almost 360 degrees.

In my headphones I heard the pilot ask what I thought of the view. I replied that it was truly magnificent, though it would be better if I could make out the details on the ground a little better. "OK," came the reply. "Tighten your seat belt and hang on". This I did and the aircraft went into a steep dive. Soon we were plunging down into a valley, only to zoom steeply upwards into the sky again. I felt like the luckiest man alive as we swooped and dived through the beautiful countryside below. All too soon, we were in a shallow descent into Naples airport. Before I left them, I was presented with a bag of cookies and cigars by those ever-smiling American fliers.

Once I had booked in at the transit camp, I was told that I would be leaving by sea for 'Blighty' in a few days. There was a small column of smoke coming from the crater of Vesuvius as I made my way into Naples to explore. The transit camp was full of men waiting for ships to take them home. Many of these men had been away for years, either fighting or in P.O.W. camps, and they were all in a mood to celebrate. Our enthusiasm was dampened when we were told to take great care and not drink too much while in Naples. There had been several incidents where servicemen who had celebrated to excess had been knocked on the head, dragged into an alley and stripped of everything they had, while the culprits disappeared in a flash.

One day the Major in charge of the camp sent for me. Lady Mountbatten, who had been very active in the British Red Cross and was involved in the sending of parcels to P.O.W.s, wished to speak to an ex P.O.W. about the value of these parcels. I had been selected to meet her.

In the early afternoon a car arrived and whisked me off to a handsome marble building on a hill overlooking Naples. The driver told me it was one of the Duke of Aosta's palaces. Once I had been introduced and fortified with several pink gins, Lady Mountbatten asked me how we prisoners felt about the Red Cross Parcels we received. She was delighted to hear from me that, as far as we were concerned, they were like manna from heaven. She in turn seemed very well-briefed as to the number of parcels sent and the total tonnage passed on to us by the Swiss Red Cross.

During our conversation she asked me if I had an interest in music, to which I answered that I certainly had. "It's your lucky day", she responded. "Would you like to see *Manon Lescaut* by Puccini?" I replied that I had never seen this opera and that it had never been performed in Sheffield. A number of seats had been allocated to her and I was invited.

Teatra San Carlo is one of the most famous opera houses in the world and two evenings later I was there. Sitting in a box, surrounded by a bevy of nurses. How lucky can a man get?

I eventually said goodbye from the deck of a troopship and was fascinated to watch how the passengers self-segregated themselves between those who had been 'at the sharp end' and those who had contrived to get through the war without hearing a shot fired in anger. The food on board was marvellous, with a full English breakfast to start the day and a seemingly endless series of meals throughout the day.

As we ate and drank our way west through the Mediterranean, past Gibraltar and into the Atlantic swell, the anticipation rose in all of us, reaching its peak as we entered the Mersey estuary, and a great cheer went up as we got our first glimpse of the Liver Building in the distance.

A final twist of fate for one of our number:

Strictly against all the safety regulations which had been drummed into us, he sat on the rail as we approached the dock. Suddenly he slipped backwards, falling into the water where, despite the throwing in of lifebelts and the attempts of the crew to reverse our progress, he was never seen again. What a tragic end.

If I have given you delight
By aught that I have done
Let me lie quiet in that night
Which shall be yours anon

And for the little, little span
The dead are borne in mind
Seek not to question other than
The books I leave behind

Rudyard Kipling

LINGUA FRANCA

After many years of rubbing shoulders with soldiers from many countries who served in the Middle East, and who spent years crowded together in the narrow confines of P.O.W. Camps, a lingua franca developed which became common to all of us.

Words in Arabic, Urdu, Italian, German, Hindi and British army slang.

Here is a selection of them with the translations:

Acqua	*Water*	Moya	*Water*
Alakeefik	*Uncaring*	Mungaria	*Food*
A swire	*A little*	Musquois	*No good*
Bandook	*Rifle*	Pawny	*Water*
Bardin	*Soon*	Peachy	*Soon*
Bint	*Girl*	Pukka	*Correct*
Bukshee	*Free, spare*	Quois	*Good*
Char	*Tea*	Sai eda	*Good day*
Coggage	*Paper*	Spare	*Mad*
Conner	*Food*	Squaddy	*Soldier*
Iggery	*Hurry up*	Stanna swire	*Half a moment*
Imshi	*Be off*	Sub cheese	*Everything*
Inta quois	*Very good*	T'man	*Good*
Juldi	*Quickly*	Wadi	*Gully*
Kooloo	*Everything*	Yallah	*Run away*
Maleesh	*Never mind*	Yimkin	*Perhaps*